P9-DHE-055

ANDERS
NYGREN

Makers of the Modern Theological Mind

Bob E. Patterson, Editor

KARL BARTH by *David L. Mueller*
DIETRICH BONHOEFFER by *Dallas M. Roark*
RUDOLF BULTMANN by *Morris Ashcraft*
CHARLES HARTSHORNE by *Alan Gragg*
WOLFHART PANNENBERG by *Don Olive*
TEILHARD DE CHARDIN by *Doran McCarty*
EMIL BRUNNER by *J. Edward Humphrey*
MARTIN BUBER by *Stephen M. Panko*
SÖREN KIERKEGAARD by *Elmer H. Duncan*
REINHOLD NIEBUHR by *Bob E. Patterson*
H. RICHARD NIEBUHR by *Lonnie D. Kliever*
ANDERS NYGREN by *Thor Hall*
GERHARD VON RAD by *James L. Crenshaw*
FRIEDRICH SCHLEIERMACHER by *C. W. Christian*
HANS KÜNG by *John Kiwiet*
PAUL TILLICH by *John Newport*
CARL F. H. HENRY by *Bob E. Patterson*

Makers of the Modern Theological Mind

Bob E. Patterson, Editor

ANDERS NYGREN

by Thor Hall

Word Books Publisher, Waco, Texas

Anders Nygren

Printed in the United States of America
ISBN 0–8499–0098–0
Library of Congress catalog card number: 78–59427

In Memory of My Father
Jens M. Hall
Master of His Trade
1897–1963

Contents

Editor's Preface

Who are the thinkers that have shaped Christian theology in our time? This series tries to answer that question by providing a reliable guide to the ideas of the men who have significantly charted the theological seas of our century. In the current revival of theology, these books will give a new generation the opportunity to be exposed to significant minds. They are not meant, however, to be a substitute for a careful study of the original works of these makers of the modern theological mind.

This series is not for the lazy. Each major theologian is examined carefully and critically—his life, his theological method, his most germinal ideas, his weaknesses as a thinker, his place in the theological spectrum, and his chief contribution to the climate of theology today. The books are written with the assumption that laymen will read them and enter into the theological dialogue that is so necessary to the church as a whole. At the same time they are carefully enough designed to give assurance to a Ph.D. student in theology preparing for his preliminary exams.

Each author in the series is a professional scholar and theologian in his own right. All are specialists on, and in some cases have studied with, the theologians about whom they write. Welcome to the series.

Bob E. Patterson, Editor
Baylor University

Preface

This book is a labor of love. This might as well be said confessionally at the start, so that the reader will understand what kind of book he has in his hands. If after reading it the reader can say the same evaluatively, I shall be satisfied that I have fulfilled at least a part of my purpose in writing.

But let me explain what I mean by love in this context—that is always important, as Nygren himself would want us to say. He more than anyone has taught us to distinguish between *eros* (love as desire, seeking love, or qualified love) and *agape* (love as gift, outgoing love, unqualified love). None of these apply here, however, as much as that third, more common Greek term *philia* (love as covenant, brotherly love, or mutual love).

In writing this book I am guided not by any desire to obtain love—what Nygren would describe as "sheer egocentricity"—or by any innocent and spontaneous wish to give love, regardless of the qualities or the value of the object—that attitude which Nygren describes as "pure or divine love." The book, instead, is an attempt to present as responsively and responsibly as possible the most important contributions which Anders Nygren has made to the thought-world of theologians in the twentieth century—to that *philadelphia* of scholarship which we now occupy on the journey between the secular city and *civitate Dei.* The presentation is not at all uncritical; it is not the product of the blind admiration of eros or the indiscriminate acceptance of agape. I write as a colleague, a brother and friend, not as a lover or a redeemer. Nygren might describe it as "critical analysis," but even that is probably too much to say. The book, after all, is more an exposition, and it is directed not to specialists but to a more general audience—the student of theology, the practicing clergyman, the thinking layman.

Anders Nygren's thought came to my attention during my seminary days in Sweden, when his *Eros and Agape* and his *Commentary on Romans* were high on our reading lists. Later, while struggling with basic presuppositional questions in graduate school at Duke University, I discovered Nygren's earlier philosophical and methodological works. I found there a theologian in search of a proper philosophical base, an appropriate scientific method, and an orientation on the essential Christian kerygma. He answered for me the question how as a theologian I could remain at one and the same time an honest twentieth-century intellectual and a committed Christian believer. Such is my personal indebtedness to this man. I have since found myself forced to go beyond the answers which I found in Nygren's earlier works—and so, by the way, has he. Nygren's most recent major work, *Meaning and Method,* shows clearly that he has continued to work on the questions that are fundamental not only to Christian thought but to Christian existence in the modern age, and he is still growing.

I first met Anders Nygren in 1962, during his extended visit to the United States. He and his wife Irmgard came to Duke University for a few days, and as a Scandinavian working on a dissertation on Lundensian theological methodology which included a chapter on Nygren's thought, I naturally sought contact. He kindly read my manuscript and—more kindly yet—affirmed my understanding. He even suggested that we "put away our titles"—his, of course, the more impressive than mine, and the suggestion was therefore a gesture no Scandinavian at the time would fail to recognize as a gracious invitation to continued friendship. My wife and I have since visited the Nygrens in Lund on numerous occasions, and especially often during my first sabbatical there in 1968–69, when Nygren was finishing his magnum opus, *Meaning and Method*, and I was writing *A Framework for Faith*. In addition we have had occasional correspondence on many subjects over the years—the saddest exchange being our condolences and his response at the death of his wife, his *innerligt älskade maka* (deeply beloved wife).

I last visited Nygren in the spring of 1977, during the time of this writing. Then in his eighty-seventh year and confined to bed because of a back ailment, he was still unmistakably himself—a gracious man, a quick wit, an artful conversationalist, and a warm friend. We discussed again some details of his thought which I find problematic and which I have pointed to in this book. We have discussed them many times; I think we understand one another.

In studying the life and work of Anders Nygren, we are fortunate to possess not only a number of biographical sketches in lexica and who's who of various kinds, but a published document from his own pen entitled "Intellectual Autobiography." This is a retrospective view of the influences and interests that have been at work at various points in his life and that have something to do with what in fact he has done in his research and writing, and in his larger academic and ecclesiastical involvements, during his career. In addition, since Nygren's life and work throughout have been both public and published, we have available to us a remarkable record which includes not only his own writings and public contributions to the ongoing debate within university and church, but the writings of others about him—critical reviews, scholarly expositions, books as well as articles, and much of this material now also available in English. Our problem is not, then, how and where to find the information we need; the challenge is rather how to limit and organize the material so as to present a full picture and yet stay within the scope and plan of the present volume.

Our approach in this book will be the following: In an introductory section, Part I, we shall take a quick look at two aspects of the chronological record, namely, the Swedish context in which Nygren's life for the most part has been set, and the biographical data as they describe Nygren's career and professional development. The main body of the book, Parts II through IV, follow with further detail and focus on various major facets of Nygren's thought, from his philosophical foundations to his primary theological emphases. In a final section, Part V, we shall seek to sum up the material by specifying what can be considered Nygren's theological character and discussing also some critical evaluations and constructive suggestions.

I am of course deeply conscious of my indebtedness to a number of people as I present this book for publication. First on the list, naturally, is Anders Nygren himself—he is the "categorical presupposition" for the existence of this book! Then, those who invited me to write and gave me the opportunity to do so: the editor of the series, Bob Patterson, the publisher, Word Books, and Word's editor Mary Ruth Howes, who also made an investment in the project; the University of Tennessee at Chattanooga, which permits me to arrange my teaching schedule so as to make possible an intensive writing period occasionally, and whose Faculty Research Committee provided funds allowing me to spend the spring and summer of 1977 in Scandinavia; and the American Philosophical Society which made a grant in support of a portion of the project, namely that which has to do with Nygren's theoretical definition of religion and its importance in the light of the issues of religious pluralism now being debated among philosophers of religion. And finally, those who helped me finish this work within a reasonable time frame—my secretary, Mrs. June Breland, who handled the main portions of this manuscript with characteristic skills; the Department's secretary, Mrs. Judy Beebe, who handled the rest; and my wife Gerd who worked hard, and with usual grace, to keep our life well sustained under the now—for us—extraordinary conditions of Scandinavian existence, and who did the bibliography.

I say to each of these and all, for all help on this project, *mange takk!*

Bövre, Summer of 1977

Part One

A THEOLOGIAN

I. His Context

A theologian does not exist in a vacuum. Neither does he emerge without being influenced by the cultural context and by those who did theology before him.

This is now generally recognized, and no elaborate arguments need to be marshaled in its defense. Logic requires the recognition that since theology is a discipline that relates both to faith and thought, and since it uses language as its primary tool, the theologian cannot do his work without reference to a community or tradition of faith, without relating to the thought forms or mind sets that characterize the larger community of men, or without learning his trade from those who formed the language and shaped the discipline before him. Universal human experience supports the same points with inexorable force: the human being is a social entity. Wisdom is a shared thing. Learning is learned.

Anders Nygren is no exception. He is a theologian in context, and the immediate context is Sweden—twentieth-century Sweden—and particularly the Swedish universities and the Swedish church. Before focusing our attention on Nygren's own contributions to the making of the modern theological mind, we must therefore have a quick introduction to the cultural setting within which his life and work have been framed. We cannot, of course, draw the picture in great detail here but must limit ourselves to describing some characteristic features in the general religious situation, in the philosophical debate, and in the theological schools of the country—features which have all had formative influence on Anders Nygren's thought.[1]

THE CULTURAL CONTEXT

It must be remembered from the start that when we talk about twentieth-century Sweden we are dealing with a country which within Nygren's lifetime has gone from an agrarian economy, a conservative political orientation, and cultural Christendom, to become a little industrial giant, a model of a modern social democracy, and a thoroughly secularized society. These developments have come so rapidly as to obscure the fact that Swedish culture has long and impressive historical roots, and they are so radical as at least in part to erase the memory of its Christian origins.

It was during the Viking Age—the ninth and tenth centuries A.D.—that Christian missionaries first came to the area from England and Germany. Endorsed at first by individual chieftains, Christianity became the religion of the land when in 1050 A.D. a Christian king was victorious over all opponents and gathered all of *Svearike* under a single throne. Thus began the close association of church and state which has continued, with various modifications, to this day. The first archbishopric—at Uppsala—was established in 1164; the first university—also at Uppsala—in 1477.

The Protestant Reformation came early to Sweden, in 1527, inspired mainly by Luther and led by one of Luther's own students at Wittenberg, the Swedish priest Olaus Petri. The national church now assumed a Lutheran confessional orientation, and Lutheran orthodoxy soon came to dominate public education as it did the church and state—the absolute monarchy. Sweden now also became a major military power in Northern Europe, separating itself from the alliance with

Denmark-Norway and gaining vast territories in Russia (Finland), Poland and Germany, as well as in what is now the southern part of Sweden, *Scania*. The university at Lund was established there in 1668.

Although Sweden has since lost most of the territories captured at that time, the country is still a major power in the North. It has developed a policy of neutrality in relation to dominant world powers and has managed to stay out of both World Wars and other conflicts in the twentieth century. Its form of government has developed from absolute monarchy to aristocracy, to constitutional monarchy, to liberal democracy, to the present-day social democracy. Rich in resources, natural and human, it has a high productivity and an impressive technology, resulting in extensive trade and an excellent living standard.

Science and the secular arts have long had a high status in Sweden. The Academy of Science was founded in 1739; the Swedish Academy in 1786. The general educational level is very high, and illiteracy and poverty are now virtually nonexistent. The mind set of the people has been broadly influenced by all the major movements of thought and sensibility that have swept through Western, especially European, culture since the Enlightenment, and although some 95 percent of the population still belong, nominally, to the Church of Sweden, the church has had to defend itself from time to time against the attacks of aggressive opponents in many camps. Lutheran orthodoxy has especially been given a hard time in Sweden in recent decades by the philosophers.

One might wonder, perhaps, why Lutheran theologians in a Lutheran country should feel themselves under obligation to answer critics and respond to opponents among the philosophers. The answer lies in the Swedish academic structure. The two theological faculties in Sweden are university faculties, set in the milieu of the secular liberal arts and the classical and modern sciences. Although they function as the church's seminaries and are responsible for the theological education of ministers in the Church of Sweden, the faculties are not under the jurisdiction of the church, neither do they speak for the church. As part of the university structure, the theological faculties are not only free to develop their views in interaction with the trends and tendencies in the academic world, but theologians are in fact challenged by academic colleagues in other fields to develop their theology so as to remain in dialogue with the arts and sciences generally. This explains much of the theological quest for scientific respectability which has characterized the faculties in Sweden especially during the twentieth century. It also explains why orthodox churchmen have come to feel that the theological faculties at times have left the fold and joined the enemies.

One should note that although Swedish intellectual and academic trends have usually developed in close interaction with German philosophical and theological "schools," this does not mean that there is no indigenous creativity in the country. Swedish scholars have never felt obliged to follow the signals of the leading centers of learning to the south in a slavish way. Both in philosophy and in theology, points of view have been developed that represent uniquely Swedish perspectives and approaches. The scholars do, of course, study the Continental masters—a period of study in Germany has in fact seemed a necessary part of the "habilitation" (process of qualifying) of Swedish professorial candidates, even to this day. But when they return home, Swedish scholars are seen to sort out their gleanings in a more individualistic manner; they tend to develop their philosophical and theological approaches along decidedly homespun lines.

THE PHILOSOPHICAL-THEOLOGICAL SCENE

At the end of the nineteenth century, the Swedish philosophical scene was dominated by Hegelian or Hegel-inspired perspectives. The philosophical authorities at the time were in the tradition of J. J. Borelius, a proponent of classical Hegelian idealism, and Christopher J. Boström, who had turned toward an idealism of a more personalistic bent. Boström, who had taught at Uppsala, was clearly the more influential of the two, although at Lund the theologians—the so-called "Great Faculty" during the middle of the nineteenth century—for a long time held to the Borelius line as being most consistent with the grand theocentric synthesis which they were hoping to produce. In time, however, most of the Swedish theologians came to feel that Boström's more nonspeculative, empirically oriented personalism was more open for interplay with the cultural and ecclesiastical emphases for which, as churchmen, they were anxious to win a hearing to a greater extent than the transcendental metaphysic of Borelius.

At the opening of the twentieth century, several new and rather different philosophical perspectives began to emerge as influential on the Swedish scene. In his intellectual autobiography, Nygren refers to the effect that a little book by J. E. Erdmann, a German proponent of the philosophy of common sense and the analysis of ordinary language, had on him as a high school student. As he expresses it, this book was for him the initiation into "the philosophical eros." Later, as a student at Lund, he was strongly influenced by a young philosopher, Torgny Segerstedt, who guided Nygren toward the preoccupation with the "scientific" [2] nature of philosophy.

At Uppsala, in the meantime, two representatives of philosophical criticism, even positivism, were in the process of altering radically the orientation of the philosophical faculty, namely, Axel Hägerström, the professor of practical philosophy, and Adolf Phalén, the professor of theoretical philosophy. Ragnar Bring, who later became Nygren's friend and colleague at Lund, studied philosophy at Uppsala under these men and was strongly influenced by their unbending criticism of philosophical idealism in any form, particularly their harsh attacks directed against metaphysical speculation and epistemological subjectivism. For him, as for Nygren, the question now became, "How is it possible to do philosophy in a nonmetaphysical manner?"

The theological faculties at Lund and Uppsala both found it difficult to relate to these new developments in philosophy. In addition, the new theological schools on the Continent—the Wellhausen school in historical-critical biblical interpretation and the Ritschl-Hermann-Harnack succession in systematic and historical dogmatics—began to demand their attention, and the theologians thus felt under pressure from both "inside" and "outside" forces to develop a response and find new ways to do theology in the twentieth century.

At Lund, the leader of the faculty at the opening of the twentieth century was a delightful, witty and articulate theologian, Pehr Eklund, who attempted to keep faith both with Lutheran orthodoxy, the Ritschlian school, and historical-critical methodology by focusing primarily on Luther-research—he found in Luther's theology the clearest possible expression of evangelical Christian faith, which he defined in Ritschlian terms as "unconditional trust in God." This unique combination of new and old has to some degree come to characterize Swedish theology in the twentieth century. There is, in fact, good reason to think that Luther-research is one of Sweden's main contributions to modern theology. At any rate, it has been an approach that has helped several generations of Swedish theologians cope with the pressures from both right and left—from the conservative confessional church community as well as the new schools in theology.

At Uppsala, the opening of the twentieth century brought the inauguration of a bright young theological professor, Nathan Söderblom, and with it the beginnings of a more self-consciously modern, scientific approach to theology. Söderblom had no difficulties with the scientific point of view—on the contrary, he affirmed it. "Not less science, but more science, and with it new humility and new strength," he said in his inaugural lecture; "theology is nothing less than the science of religion." For Söderblom the scientific interest of the theologian manifested itself in two directions: first the history of religions, second the psychology of religion. In fact, Söderblom's approach to theology represented nothing less than a radical reorientation of the Swedish theological community; from now on theologians directed themselves to a series of new objects, by way of new methods—considering new materials in new ways. The primary objects of study were now the historical religions and human religious experiences; and the methods that were utilized tied the theologians in with the empirical, historical, philosophical and psychological sciences generally. Not all Swedish theologians spanned the entire spectrum of Söderblom's scientific theology, of course. Söderblom's work actually became the inspiration for two different and distinct traditions that can be observed to develop in Swedish theology in the twentieth century—what we might call the Aulén line, centered at Lund, and what we might call the Runestam line, most evident at Uppsala. The first sought to establish the scientific respectability of theology by way of philosophical and historical perspectives; the second sought to do the same by way of sociological and psychological inquiries. We shall return to these in a minute.

In the meantime we must mention another Uppsala scholar who has made a distinct contribution to the development of Swedish theology in the twentieth century, namely, Söderblom's younger colleague at the university, Einar Billing. Billing was more of a Boströmian idealist than Söderblom, and his use of the scientific method—particularly the historians' research procedures—was therefore clearly directed toward the construction of a grand historical-theological synthesis, history interpreted as a divine drama. In addition to a strong concern for the development of historiological perspectives that were applicable to the work of the theologian—perspectives that have been further developed by Gustaf Aulén, Anders Nygren and Ragnar Bring at Lund—Billing was also concerned that the theologian not be limited to a historical-descriptive or even an analytical task. Billing felt that he must finally pose the question of ultimate truth and try to see the ordinary and relative historical events within the larger realities of an absolute transcendent drama. In this, Billing put himself on collision course with Hägerström and Phalén, the Uppsala philosophers who were the devout critics of every tendency toward metaphysics and subjectivity, and the Lundensians chose not to follow Billing in that direction. In their view theology ought to proceed along the lines of historical-critical research and on the presuppositions of philosophical criticism itself. Billing's followers at Uppsala, on the other hand, Arvid Runestam, Torsten Bohlin, and Hjalmar Lindroth, did accept Billing's more idealistic-apologetic approach. We have thus identified a second point that divides the Aulén line and the Runestam line in modern Swedish theology.

THE TWO LINES

When Gustaf Aulén moved from Uppsala, where he had been Söderblom's assistant, to the professorship at Lund, in 1913, he was already convinced that theology must establish its scientific respectability in the modern age by way of the historical-critical methodology, not in dependence on Boström's or any other form of idealism. Aulén had experienced the beginnings of Hägerström's and Phalén's intellectual revolution at Uppsala, and he was well aware of the corrosive effect of their views on all kinds of metaphysical philosophy and subjectivistic theology. He was not, however, himself a philosopher. His interests focused primarily on the investigation and exposition of historical Christian faith.[3] The principal discussion of philosophical and methodological matters was left to Aulén's younger colleagues at Lund, Anders Nygren and Ragnar Bring. Within two decades these two men developed a theological methodology that was designed to withstand the criticism of the Uppsala positivists and relate Swedish theology, especially systematic theology, to the requirements of the modern age. So emphatic were they, in fact, in the commitment to this cause, that they actually joined the philosophical critics of theology in their efforts to sniff out the metaphysical and subjectivistic elements in the works of their theological colleagues, past and present, Swedish and foreign. Especially sharp was the Lundensian criticism of their colleagues to the north, at Uppsala, namely Runestam, Bohlin, and Lindroth. These men now felt themselves under double attack—from the philosophers at Uppsala and the theologians at Lund—and a break was inevitable. It came in the early 1930s, when Runestam left the editorial committee of *Svensk teologisk kvartalskrift* after a tense methodological dispute with Aulén. The bifurcation among the disciples of Söderblom and Billing was now complete, and Swedish theology settled into a period of internal squabbles between an Uppsala faction—the Runestam line, and a Lund faction—the Aulén line.

Arvid Runestam, who was a close follower of the psychological emphases of Söderblom and the synthetic apologetics of Billing, emerged on the Swedish scene as a confessed disciple of Wilhelm Herrmann. He was convinced that the challenges of the Hägerström camp could best be met by way of an entirely different and distinct epistemology—a theory of knowledge which was based on psychological inquiries into the peculiar nature of faith, or as he himself expressed it, by a "science of faith" which constitutes "an understanding psychology applied to a God-believing subject." [4] Basic to Runestam's perspective is the distinction, which he had learned from Billing and Herrmann, between "self-realization" and "self-reflection." To him these two concepts stand for two altogether separate and autonomous ways of understanding things. Both are scientifically valid, but self-realization (the religious method) is far superior to self-reflection (the scientific method) in that it is capable of penetrating to significantly deeper levels of understanding and giving the believer deeper insights into the true meaning of things. Runestam claims, in other words, that when the reality that is to be investigated lies deeper than the factual evidence that can be approached by way of observation and objective analysis—when one deals with the level of experiential reality—then there is need for a more profound method of investigation, a deeper psychology. Theology, the science of religion, cannot allow itself to be reduced to the level of ordinary science; it has before it an extraordinary object of inquiry, namely religious consciousness, and it must therefore approach it with an extraordinary method of inquiry, a scientific approach that allows access to, and understanding of, this unique and extraordinary object. Runestam describes his method this way:

> The scientist [of religion] tries to place himself within the self-realizing individual's standpoint and to observe him, not as an object among other objects that may be analyzed and described, but as a living, willing, knowing, and acting subject. . . . He has, in a sense, to have a secondary involvement in the self-realizing individual's situation—a secondary self-realization—while at the same time keeping himself in the primary self-realization's attitude.[5]

Runestam's methodology was considered a serious tactical blunder by Aulén and his colleagues at Lund, and for two reasons: On the one hand it was evident that Runestam tried to establish the scientific respectability of theology by applying the perspectives of psychology to the investigation of the theologian's object of study—a procedure which placed theology in danger of being swallowed up by psychology and losing its own individuality and integrity as a discipline. On the other hand, in order to retain any special role for the theologian, Runestam was forced to claim that the theologian's object of study is inaccessible to ordinary psychological perspectives and that only those who are themselves participants of the religious consciousness in question can understand its meaning—a point of view which is fraught with the obvious metaphysical and subjectivistic tendencies which caused the theologian's claim to scientific respectability to get stranded in the first place. It was precisely in order to avoid these methodological traps that the Lundensian group decided to build a theological method on the foundations of philosophical criticism and along the lines of historical-critical research. In their view, this would be the only possible way of securing for theology the status of a scientific discipline.

Anders Nygren's contributions to the development of this Lundensian methodology are of fundamental importance, not only to the Swedish philosophical and theological debate, but to the making of the modern theological mind as a whole. It will be one of the major tasks of the chapters that follow to assist the reader in the understanding of this dimension of Nygren's thought.

THEOLOGICAL CONCERNS

There is another dimension of the Swedish theological situation in the twentieth century to which we must refer as background for the study of Anders Nygren. Swedish theologians in this century have been concerned not only with methodological issues or with the attempt to give their discipline a sound theoretical basis in the face of philosophical and scientific challenges; they have also been committed to the recovery of essential Christian emphases and the correction of what they consider to be the theological mistakes of the past and the present. This is in fact an emphasis that has gone like a dominant gene from man to man in the succession of theologians to which Anders Nygren belongs.

Pehr Eklund may be said to have begun this recovery process when he insisted on the orientation of theology around the concept of "the purely evangelical." His point was directed against a series of distortions of Christian faith and life which he found exemplified among the theologians of the past, particularly—as he describes it—"the scholastic-orthodox-legalistic," "the intellectualistic-rationalistic-theoretical," and "the emotionalistic-pietistic-romantic" understanding of the faith. In attacking the first of these, Eklund could sound positively liberal; when he took up the second, his own conservative notes seemed to prevail; and when he confronted the third, he could appear at times rather reactionary. His own interpretation of the evangelical Christian faith contained, as we have seen, particular elements of Ritschlian theology, Lutheran confessionalism, and biblical—especially Pauline—thought; it was in many ways a unique liberal-conservative construct.

The same interest in genuine Christianity—"the genuinely religious, the characteristically Christian, the purely evangelical"—and the same complex theological orientation characterized the work of Nathan Söderblom and Einar Billing as well. Söderblom was primarily concerned to identify the distinguishing marks of the Christian religion as religion, which he did by way of a series of sharp conceptual contrasts: natural versus prophetic religions, cultural versus revelational religion, general versus special revelation, anthropocentric versus theocentric faith, and infinity mysticism versus personality mysticism as the nature of religious life. Christianity was consistently placed in the second of the two columns.[6] Billing continued this study in contrasts by setting over against one another the Greek and the Christian, the cyclical and the dramatic-linear concepts of history.[7] For both Söderblom and Billing, the Christian message was characterized by what they described as dualism—though not the metaphysical dichotomy of nature and spirit which was typical of Greek thought. Christian dualism was of a "practical, ethical, religious" kind; it represented a perspective on history—an interpretation of history as a dramatic struggle between God and his enemies, between the powers of destruction and God's will to save. On the one side stand the devil, self, sin, and death; on the other, God, faith, grace, and eternal life. In its essence the drama takes shape as a continuing confrontation between egocentricity and theocentricity.

By the time he started his teaching career at Lund, Gustaf Aulén had already entered into the tradition from Eklund, Söderblom and Billing with a conscious commitment to the task of identifying and explicating the unique character of Christian faith.[8] This commitment expressed itself both in his lifelong interest in the history of dogma and in his own presentation of a systematic theology, *The Faith of the Christian Church*. The theologian's task, according to Aulén, is to investigate the Christian faith in its historical givenness, to bring to light its characteristic affirmations and to explicate their theological significance. As he studied the history of doctrine, however, Aulén became convinced that the evangelical faith had found clear expression only in certain limited periods and contexts. At other times and in other contexts it had been obscured and distorted beyond recognition. Aulén was particularly happy with the theology of the New Testament, certain early fathers, and the Protestant Reformation. Medieval scholasticism, post-reformation orthodoxy, and modern rationalism, on the other hand, caused him concern.

In regard to the twentieth century, Aulén considered it especially important to counteract the influence of the Ritschlian "school," most especially Harnack, and to recover certain essential evangelical emphases in the face of the historicism, individualism, and moralism which he found characteristic of nineteenth-century theology as a whole. In his view, there were three emphases which were typical of the gospel, the early church fathers, and the Protestant Reformation which must now be recovered: the dynamic-dramatic understanding of history, the conception of Christian life as life in community, and the interpretation of faith as a theocentric God-relationship. Aulén considered it the peculiar task of the new theologians at Lund to emphasize these points in opposition to orthodox dogmatism, pietistic exclusiveness, and humanistic idealism.

It is with these theological concerns—emphases which unite Uppsala and Lund in the quest for theological recovery—that Anders Nygren identifies himself as he comes to take up his own theological task. One may describe these concerns as part of the neoorthodox motif in Swedish theology in the twentieth century. Many interpreters have in fact considered the Lundensians as Sweden's counterpart to the Barthians on the European Continent,[9] and there are certainly a number of obvious parallels present. But Swedish neoorthodoxy, particularly as it found form in Lund, is of a fundamentally different brand from that propounded by a Barth and a Brunner.[10]

In the orientation on the theocentric character of evangelical Christian faith, the Lundensians are surely in full harmony with the intentions of Continental neoorthodoxy. But in the understanding of the theological task, and in relation to the philosophical and cultural context of theology, the Lundensians are definitely neither Barthian nor Brunnerian. Not only do the Lundensians take a different view of philosophy and of the relationship of philosophy and theology; they attach themselves to a particular philosophical perspective—namely, philosophical criticism—which Continental neoorthodoxy considers more or less useless. While Barthian neoorthodoxy developed along *dialectic* lines, Lundensian neoorthodoxy entered into a relationship of *dialog* with critical philosophy and scientific theory. Thus, in confronting the weaknesses of modern theology, the Lundensians did not seek to retreat from the modern intellectual and cultural developments to the unchallenged theological positions of an earlier day and time. They wanted to develop a theology which combined the concern for the recovery of essential Christian emphases with the equally significant task of establishing theology as a modern scientific discipline.

The main problem of contemporary theology, according to the Swedish tradition into which Anders Nygren entered, is how and in what sense Christian theology can be made to become both positively Christian and strictly scientific. It was in the solution of this problem that Anders Nygren came to make his most important contributions to the making of the modern theological mind.

II. His Life

Anders Nygren's life is a long and full one—spanning all of what we have yet seen of the twentieth century, and the decade before it; including long and significant careers in both university and church, in scholarship and ministry; involving both national and international, ecclesiastical as well as political concerns; all of it enclosed in an extensive period of preparation at the beginning and an equally extensive season of retirement at the end; yet most of it with home base in a small university town in the Southern part of Sweden, Lund. The biographical facts are extensive and impressive by themselves. But Nygren is an intellectual, and the facts are therefore all entangled in thought. We shall need to study his life not merely from the standpoint of dates and facts, but in the light of Nygren's self-understanding and self-reflection as well.[1]

STAGES ON LIFE'S WAY

Anders Theodor Samuel Nygren was born in Gothenburg, Sweden, on November 15, 1890, the third son of Samuel Nygren, then principal of the Elementary Teacher's College and inspector of elementary schools in that city, and his wife Anna

Maria, born Lundström. Nygren has had little to say about his mother except that she was a profoundly devout Christian person who yet provided for a rich and inclusive cultural atmosphere in the home. His father obviously was the dominant figure in young Nygren's life—a man who, although he died when Anders was fifteen, left his son with an indelible impression of personal and professional integrity which came to have lasting effect on young Nygren's life, from the beginning.

Samuel Nygren was a graduate of the University of Lund, with degrees in theology as well as philosophy obtained under the influence of the so-called "Great Faculty" in the early 1860s. This was the time of the idealistic cultural-ecclesiastical synthesis inspired by Hegelian philosophy, and the older Nygren seems to have aspired to make a contribution to its establishment by preparing himself for an academic appointment. However, for financial reasons he was forced to discontinue his university career and take up teaching, partly in the *realgymnasium* (College of Natural Science) in Gothenburg, and partly at the Teacher's College, where after fifteen years as *adjunkt* he became principal in 1887. An intellectual and a devout churchman, he was an active participant in both public worship and theological debate. It was in his father's library that young Nygren found the book by Erdmann that became his first introduction to philosophical analysis. It was in his father's selection of materials for family devotions that the son was introduced to the excitement of Luther's writings and the intricacies of Paul's theology. It was in his father's conversations that Anders was first made aware of the extraordinary character of Christian agape. It was in the company of his father, as a twelve-year-old observer at a grand theological debate in the Gothenburg diocese, that young Nygren first learned of the different theories and interpretations of the Christian doctrine of the atonement. And it was together with his parents, attending public worship at the cathedral, that he got to know the Christian faith and life, as he himself expresses it, "from within."

At the death of his father in 1906, Anders Nygren's family moved to Lund, where he and his two brothers in due course became students at the university. Anders spent the first two and a half years at the cathedral school, then began his philosophical and theological studies, receiving his *teol. cand.* degree, including *practicum*, in 1912.[2] His main interest during these first years at the university were philosophy of religion and systematic theology, but the study of the New Testament also held a certain attraction for Nygren. He was especially interested in the Epistle to the Romans, undertaking a comparative study of a number of commentaries while seeking to develop a systematic view of Paul's message. His first love, however, was philosophy of religion, then a subcategory of the history of religions and taught by a young *docent*, Torgny Segerstedt. It was in conversations with Segerstedt that Nygren's future research program was developed. Segerstedt advised him to focus on philosophy of religion—the scientifically defensible approach to theology—and to avoid dogmatics and ethics, the metaphysical and unscientific disciplines. Nygren rejected the notion of a philosophy of religion which would serve as substitute for theology as representing a theoretical travesty; such a philosophy would immediately run into criticism for being itself metaphysical and unscientific, and Nygren wanted none of it. Instead he made it his goal to develop a purely scientific, nonmetaphysical philosophy of religion as well as to lay a scientific basis for dogmatics and moral theology.

Nygren was ordained in 1912, twenty-one years old, and assigned to the pastorate at Bokenäs in the Gothenburg Diocese. After a year he moved to the parish of Ölmevalla, where he remained until 1920, later serving for a short period in Stångby and Vallkärra. Parish duties did not prevent him from continuing his studies, however; on the contrary, his early years in the ministry were in fact a time of concentration. Nygren found preaching and scholarship to be mutually supportive—both led to preoccupation with the central truths of Christian faith. Even philosophy and philosophical analysis of religion, when approached in a critical manner, assist in clarifying the essential meaning of the minister's message. Nygren was particularly engaged with the philosophical issues involved in the theoretical definition of the nature of religion, especially the perspectives raised by Ernst Troeltsch and Rudolf Otto in their analyses of the religious a priori; he was writing a doctoral dissertation on the subject, seeking to develop a nonmetaphysical, critical-analytical approach to the definition of the religious category of experience.

During the later stages of that project, in 1920, Nygren made a journey to Germany to discuss his work with Troeltsch and Otto, Carl Stange and others. It was a richly rewarding trip, not least because he found something he was *not* looking for, his wife. Irmgard Helene Luise Brandin had herself been a student of Troeltsch at Berlin; she helped Nygren prepare his views in German for discussion with her former teacher, while he—Nygren—sought to prepare her for a lifelong sojourn in Sweden. They were married a year later and formed a partnership of heart and mind which lasted for more than fifty years, until her death. Irmgard became Nygren's sounding board and translator. Together they had four children, two boys and two girls. The sons are both academicians: Ingemar, an *adjunkt* like his grandfather; Gotthard, professor of systematic theology like his father; the daughters are both married to ministers, themselves brothers, both well-known men in the Swedish church.

When Nygren presented his dissertation in 1921, he was immediately made *docent* in philosophy of religion. His duties involved a series of lectures, as well as the leadership of certain catechetical exercises in the practical-theological division, and in fulfilling these responsibilities Nygren experienced some of his most productive years. He published several additional books, one on the scientific foundations of theology, another on philosophical and Christian ethics. In 1924 he was made one of two professors of systematic theology at Lund, the other being Gustaf Aulén. At the time, Ragnar Bring had also transferred to Lund and was studying for his *teol. cand.* degree. He attended Nygren's lectures, and the two became close friends. It was through Bring that Nygren now became acquainted with the Uppsala philosophy, and it was in Bring he found his closest collaborator in the endeavors to establish a sound philosophical foundation and an appropriate scientific method for theology. When Aulén became a bishop of the church in 1933, Bring—who had been Aulén's *docent* a while earlier—was brought back from Åbo, Finland, to assume the other chair in systematic theology. Nygren and Bring thus came to work side by side until Nygren's own elevation to the episcopacy in 1948. The close friendship between Aulén, Nygren and Bring has in fact lasted to this day—into Aulén's ninety-ninth year, Nygren's eighty-eighth year, and Bring's eighty-third.

Nygren's twenty-four years of tenure as professor were rich and full years indeed. Having worked his way through the philosophical and methodological issues during the early 1920s, he proceeded to do theology in the scientific manner. The method that he had developed, described as "motif research," was now applied to the most central concept of Christianity—love. Nygren wanted to analyze this concept from a historical-critical perspective and clear out some of the confusion that is attached to it. Especially important, he thought, was the task of clarifying the interaction and interrelationships of the Greek concept of *eros* and the Christian concept of *agape* throughout the history of Christian thought. It was a mammoth-sized undertaking, requiring extensive and tedious inquiries into the various periods of Christian doctrine and the thought of all the major theologians of the past, and Nygren spent the better part of ten years on the project. It resulted in a two-volume work, entitled *Den kristna kärlekstanken genom tiderna: Eros och agape* (English title, *Agape and Eros*), first published in 1930–36 and later in four additional Swedish editions, two English editions, two Japanese editions, and translations into six other languages. The work is undoubtedly one of the classics of Christian theology, and certainly—as Aulén says—"one of the most noteworthy theological books in this century."[3]

Toward the end of the 1930s, Nygren once more shifted his attention in new directions—or returned, rather, to another of his original concerns, the Epistle to the Romans. By this time there had developed a strong sense of partnership between systematic theologians and biblical scholars in Sweden, notably between Bring and Nygren on the one hand and Johannes Lindblom, Hugo Odeberg (both at Lund), and Anton Fridrichsen (at Uppsala) on the other. These men cooperated in the planning of a new series of biblical commentaries, originally conceived by Nygren and structured on the principles of historical-systematic analysis, which was to combine the insights of scientific biblical scholarship and the perspectives of biblical theology in a systematic presentation of New Testament thought. Nygren's contribution to the series, a volume on Romans, was published in 1943 and immediately established Nygren as a masterful interpreter of Pauline theology.

Several other facets of Nygren's professorship at Lund must be mentioned here. He was instrumental in the founding of the Lund Philosophical Society, and served as its first president from 1922 to 1926. He was chairman of the Theological Association from 1924 to 1931, and later served for many years as president of Lund Theological Society. As a member of the theological faculty, Nygren was also a participant in the Cathedral Chapter, the governing body of the Lund Diocese, and a representative to the General Church Council of the Church of Sweden. He soon became involved in international and ecumenical concerns as well. Following several visits to Germany during the early years of the Nazi takeover, Nygren wrote a series of articles exposing various aspects of the new regime. His essays on the German church struggle during 1933 and 1934 were also published in book form and translated into English and Dutch—though not into German. The book nevertheless resulted in a *Reise und Redeverbot* (ban on travel and public speech) for the author in Germany. With the collapse of the Third Reich in 1945, however, Nygren became one of the first theological scholars from abroad to visit Germany and lecture to audiences both West and East starved for contact with the outside world. He also traveled to England to give extensive lecture series to the German theological students and faculty imprisoned at Norton Camp—and was honored by the conferral of a *Doctor Captivitatis* for his kindness.

Nygren's ecumenical involvements had already begun in

1927, when he represented the Church of Sweden at the Faith and Order Conference at Lausanne. Ten years later, at the Edinburgh conference of the same group, Nygren was commissioned, together with the Danish church historian Professor Jens Nörregaard, to give some lectures clarifying the role of Lutheranism in ecumenical contexts. Nygren's own role at that conference was an important one; his paper served, in fact, to direct the attention of the first Section entitled "The Grace of Our Lord Jesus Christ" to the central point of the gospel—and its report, thereby, to complete unanimity. Later the section's views were unanimously adopted by the full assembly. Nygren continued the same role at Amsterdam in 1948 and at the next Faith and Order Conference at Lund in 1952. By that time he had also become president of the Lutheran World Federation and spoke with authority of his church's orientation on the central point of the gospel and of the unity which the church has already been given in Christ. For Nygren, "the way to unity is the way to the center."

At the Lund conference, Nygren was made chairman of the European Section of the Theological Commission on Christ and His Church. Charged with the task of explicating the ecumenical implications of baptism in the church's struggle for unity, the Section presented its report at the next meeting of Faith and Order in New Haven, 1957, but found itself shot down—as Nygren says, because of the fact that it had not focused on the central meaning of baptism. Three years later, at St. Andrews, the story was different. Now the Commission presented a study of the meaning of baptism based on a Christological starting point and anchored in biblical exegesis, and once more unanimity was reached—Nygren's motto was proven true, "The way to unity is the way to the center." Nygren has been guided by the same conviction in all of the ecumenical contexts in which he has been involved, in conversations within the Lutheran camp as well as in dialogue with Reformed, Anglican, and Roman Catholic theologians.

Two additional phases of Nygren's life must be accounted for at this point: his episcopacy and his retirement. Nygren had been offered several bishoprics over the years of his professorship, but he had always declined out of regard for his obligations as a scholar and teacher. Then in 1948 the Lund diocese was vacated, and Nygren was again the choice. His scholarship had already suffered because of extensive travels; the presidency of the Lutheran World Federation and his other ecumenical involvements promised to distract him further in the years ahead. Moreover, this was Lund, the diocese in which he had lived and participated for twenty-five years, and the pastoral ministry was after all his first love. Nygren decided to accept, and went into another season not only of life but of his authorship as well. During the eleven years of his episcopacy, several minor but significant books came from his pen, among them his *Herdabrev,* translated into English under the title *The Gospel of God,* and his lectures on church unity, *Kristus och hans kyrka* (*Christ and His Church*), translated and published in Germany, England, America, and Finland. He continued to travel and lecture extensively, and received honorary degrees from colleges and universities in Hungary, Germany, Scotland, Canada, and the United States.

Nygren retired from the office of bishop in 1959 and moved from the official residence next to the university library back to his own home two blocks away. He immediately resumed his scholarly work, returning to the questions of philosophical and theological method which had engaged him forty years earlier. He had planned for some time to write a definitive work on the analytical-critical philosophy of religion but had not found the leisure. In the meantime, new developments in philosophy had confirmed the wisdom of Nygren's perspectives and strengthened his commitment to the analysis of validity, presuppositions, language, contexts, and meaning. Nygren was especially intrigued by the works of Ludwig Wittgenstein, whom he described as "perhaps the foremost thinker of our age," and by the new Anglo-American philosophers inspired by Wittgenstein's analysis of language. During an eighteen-month visit to the United States, partly as visiting professor at the University of Minnesota, partly as resident scholar at the Ecumenical Institute in Evanston and visiting professor at the Chicago Divinity School, Nygren took opportunity to study these new trends in language analysis. His book, *Meaning and Method, Prolegomena to a Scientific Philosophy of Religion and a Scientific Theology*, was published in 1972 in England and America, simultaneously. It is a massive work, and represents an up-to-date, mature and systematic presentation of Nygren's philosophical and methodological position. It secures for Nygren a central place in the philosophical and theological debate for decades to come.

Nygren's retirement has otherwise had its ups and downs. The publication in 1970 of a critical analysis of his philosophy and theology, written by a group of European and American scholars and edited by Charles W. Kegley, was definitely an encouragement. His own failing health and the death of Irmgard, his wife and steady companion, were heavy burdens to bear. The estrangement between Nygren and his successor, Gustaf Wingren, has caused him to feel somewhat isolated from the faculty at the University, but his reputation abroad continues to increase. And he continues to work. With the help of a Finnish assistant, Miss P. Ahonen, his papers are now being prepared for deposition at the university library in Lund, and Miss Ahonen is commissioned by the Lutheran World Federation and by the Finish Academy of Science to write a definitive biography of Anders Nygren. The work should be forthcoming within a few years. In the meantime, we are sure that Nygren's selection for inclusion in the present series is very gratifying to him.

REFLECTIONS ALONG THE WAY

We have mentioned some of the factors that have contributed to giving shape and direction to Anders Nygren's life and work. To discover the real thread in all of this we must follow the leading lines in Nygren's own self-reflection along the way. We shall analyze the various facets of Nygren's thought in some detail below. At this point we must seek to identify those commitments which have informed his decisions and determined the orientation of his work and thought throughout. Nygren has himself been quite explicit about these commitments.

First and foremost stands his commitment to approach the study of Christian faith *from within.* It is important to note that with all his emphasis on scientific objectivity, and with his strong opposition to epistemological exclusiveness and subjectivity, Nygren is still anxious to emphasize that the full meaning of the Christian faith and life can only be understood by one who identifies himself personally with that faith and has experienced something of that life for himself. Such personal religious awareness is not only religiously significant; it is "a tremendous gain," Nygren says, "even on the purely intellectual level."[5] It may not be an absolute requirement for a scientific theology per se, but it is clearly of benefit to the theologian to have that psychological empathy with the subject matter that is studied which can only be derived from being a participant in that faith and life for himself.

Nygren secondly emphasizes the importance of studying the Christian faith *critically.* He was early intrigued by certain theological discussions which he witnessed as a boy. His father, in a conversation with a friend, once said, "But Christian *agape* means something quite different."[6] This triggered his interest in finding out precisely what sort of thing this agape might be. He was early made aware of Paul's struggle against the gnostic distortions of the gospel, and he was forever after interested in clearing up the effects of this and any other "foreign" influence which may have affected the interpretation of essential Christian truth. As a twelve-year-old boy, sitting in the visitors' gallery during a theological debate over the doctrine of the atonement, Nygren was fascinated by the detailed examination of theological concepts like "*hilasterion*" (Christ as "the mercy seat"), and wondered then and later who among the scholars had understood Paul correctly. In reading Erdmann as a young man, he was excited by the philosophical analysis of the conceptual traps and logical paradoxes which are so richly illustrated in the history of ideas. The book gave him what he calls his "organizing principle" for subsequent ventures into philosophy, namely, a wide analytical-critical perspective that would free him from the narrow-mindedness and "stupidity" of "peeping at the world through his own little keyhole." [7]

Nygren also became committed to *defend the integrity of Christian faith* against attacks from various opponents. At the time of his arrival in Lund, and during his years as a student, a series of public religious debates was taking place in the city featuring Bengt Lidforss and Magnus Pfannenstill, the first representing the scientific world view, the second a quiet, logical defense of the religious perspective. Nygren was a silent bystander to these debates, but he was obviously influenced by what was going on. What impressed him most was Lidforss's unwillingness or inability to understand theological statements in their own contexts or on the basis of their own presuppositions; this struck Nygren as a most unscientific approach by the champion of the scientific standpoint. Pfannenstill's defense, on the other hand, appealed to Nygren by its clear awareness of the autonomy of the religious perspective. He already saw the outlines of a new kind of apologetic based on a radical acknowledgment of the requirements of the scientific perspective and on respect for every variety of thought and language, theology included. He became determined to clear up the confusion which attaches both to the scientific critique of religion and to much of the traditional defense of the faith. Later, having taken over Pfannenstill's chair at the university, Nygren had opportunity to play the role of defender in public debates with Ingemar Hedenius, then the vociferous proponent of scientism.

The key to Nygren's own perspective is his commitment to keep both philosophy and theology *scientific*. For him, however, this did not mean that particular sciences such as the natural sciences should set the standard for what is acceptable in philosophy and theology, but that all these disciplines should be pursued in accordance with scientific principles that were generally recognized and universally applicable. What is involved in laying the foundations for a scientific philosophy and a scientific theology is a fundamental analysis of the presuppositions of science, i.e., of human knowledge, and this would once again need to be done critically—by way of principal investigations into the varieties of human awareness and human experience. Nygren thus became committed to the inquiry into the nature of science and to the task of formulating a philosophy of religion and a theological method which were in tune with the requirements of critical epistemology.

Axiomatic for Nygren in the search for the presuppositions of science was that these must be approached *in an analytical, not in a metaphysical manner*. He was convinced that what had caused problems for philosophy and theology all along was the tendency to start with certain arbitrary metaphysical assumptions. No science could be established on such foundations. Metaphysics is speculative, unverifiable, uncritical; analysis, on the other hand, deals with what is empirically given within man's actual experience and knowledge, and seeks to identify the presuppositions which are at work in the various areas or dimensions of awareness. Nygren learned the rudiments of this analytical approach from Kant and Schleiermacher, yet he was anxious to disassociate himself from both of these men; his attachment to Kant and Schleiermacher was only a question of "taking up a specific, carefully delimited line of thought which could be made fruitful in the attempt to lay a scientific, methodologically valid foundation for philosophy and theology." [8] From Kant he learned "the transcendental analytical method," or as Nygren preferred to describe it, "the logical analysis of presuppositions"; and from Schleiermacher he learned to consider religion a distinctive form of experience, categorically different from theoretical knowledge, aesthetic taste, and ethical will.

It is at this point that Nygren's analysis of the *religious a priori* comes into view. The subject had been raised by Troeltsch and Otto—but in the interest of defining the essence and content of religion, not simply to delimit the nature of religion formally and identify the categorical presuppositions which lie behind its many different historical manifestations. The latter became Nygren's goal. In the analysis of religious experience, he thought, one must seek to penetrate the actual content of religious traditions and types and seek to understand what it is that gives religion its form and meaning, its autonomy and integrity. In general, or in regard to religion as a whole, this is done in the analytical philosophy of religion; in regard to the individual religions or religious types it is done by way of historical-systematic theological investigations described by Nygren as "motif research."

Motif research is actually the methodological expression of Nygren's commitment to study theology critically. Religious motifs are nothing but the ideas, beliefs and sentiments that are part of the structure of meaning that characterizes a particular religion. These motifs are in fact, in each individual religion, structured around a *grundmotiv*, a basic or central motif which gives form and shape and content to all the rest. To understand a certain religion, it is necessary to understand its *grundmotiv*, its basic idea; to understand Christianity, it is necessary to inquire into the essential character of the Christian gospel.

For Nygren the essence of Christianity is centered in *Christology*, and Christology has its focus in the revelation of God's active, judging, and fellowship-creating *love*, agape. From the beginning, the Christian message had a definite theocentric structure, Nygren found; it was oriented on the creative, covenantal, redemptive and consummative activity of God. In the course of time, however, it had been influenced by certain other motif-structures, particularly the Greek, anthropocentric, even egocentric concept of the God-relationship. The Christian *grundmotiv* had thus been twisted and distorted and made virtually unrecognizable at various points in the history of theology. It became Nygren's goal to undertake a critical-systematic analysis of the history of the Christian idea of love, to uncover what had happened to it, and to restructure the concept of agape in its original purity. Motif research became Nygren's own "way to the center."

But the way to the center became for Nygren also the way to the *original witnesses* to the meaning of the Christ-event, the

New Testament writers, and especially to Paul. The closest Nygren ever comes to the presentation of a systematic theology is actually in the interpretation of Paul's Epistle to the Romans. Nygren thus counteracts the notion, made popular by Harnack, that the essence of Christianity lies in the simple ideas of Jesus of Nazareth, not in the elaborate theological constructs of the great apostle. Nygren not only finds the seeds of Paul's theology deep in the message of Jesus; he shows that Paul has developed a theology which unites within itself the new that is revealed in Christ and the old that is contained in the Old Testament, and that Paul has thus managed in a systematic way to express the Christian understanding of God's revelation, the activity of God's agape from beginning to end, in its original purity.

Nygren is convinced that the same purity in the presentation of the gospel is present *in Luther*. But Nygren's attachment to Luther is not a matter of confessional obedience or denominational pride. Lutheranism, he says, "does not consist of abstruse doctrines, but of simple Christian faith." [9] Luther was right only insofar as he was true to the gospel of Christ and expressed the essential Christian truth of God's agape in its original purity. Nygren also reminds the Lutheran churches that they are not a sect, a group of like-minded people committed to a definitive creed; they are "the churches of the Reformation gathered around the Gospel that belongs to the whole Church on earth." [10]

It is in line with this central orientation around the gospel that Nygren enters into *his ecumenical commitments*. At the Amsterdam Assembly in 1948 he startled his colleagues by refusing to accept the division of the church into two separate blocks, Catholic and Protestant, the one characterized by the concept of the continuity of revelation, the other by the concept of discontinuity. Nygren, then president of the Lutheran World Federation, demonstrated the untenable nature of this distinction by announcing that he must in this regard attach himself to the "Catholic" side, namely, the idea that "Christ is present in his Church, not as an occasional event now and then, but always, to the end of time." [11] Nygren thus anchors his ecclesiology in Christology, and his ecumenical activities were consequently not so much an attempt to bring about the unity of the churches separated by tradition and polity and organization as to manifest the unity which the Church has already been given in Christ. He sees it to be the particular role of Lutheranism in all ecumenical contexts "constantly to point to the center, Christ alone." [12]

One final commitment must be acknowledged as foundational to Nygren's life and work: his *dedication to the ministry of the church.* Throughout his life he had been motivated by concerns for the ministry; his philosophy and theology were always directed to helping the church understand its message rightly and communicate the gospel truthfully. When the call to the episcopacy came, therefore, Nygren was finally persuaded that he must also be willing to give himself in the active service of the church as it serves the gospel, and thus unite in his own praxis the two ministries which in theory he had held together all along. In a moving postscript to his "Intellectual Autobiography," Nygren writes:

> Theologian and minister—in the service of scholarship and of the Church! In the midst of human life with all its richness and all its tragedy, the Gospel of Jesus Christ is heard, God's "yes" to his mankind, giving them a new beginning and a new hope. The theologian interprets and the minister proclaims the gospel. Here is a twofold vocation for which one cannot help but be grateful.[13]

Part Two

IN SEARCH OF A PROPER BASE

III. Philosophy as Analysis

When in 1970 I presented my study of the Lundensian theological methodology, *A Framework for Faith,* I made the comment that while Anders Nygren must be said to be the most original thinker in the Lundensian circle, being the initiator of many of its most characteristic philosophical and methodological emphases, Ragnar Bring could well be judged the more complete methodologian, since he had extended Nygren's perspectives in two directions: inward, in reference to the elementary problems of epistemology, and outward, in regard to the practical problems of systematic theology.[1] This judgment must now be revised. With the publication of Nygren's magnum opus, *Meaning and Method,* the situation is changed. With this work, Nygren himself has extended his perspectives both backwards and forwards—into the fundamental issues of philosophy as well as toward the various philosophical and theological alternatives which are in evidence on the modern scene.

Nygren's book is primarily designed as an explication of the prolegomena of a scientific philosophy of religion—and his preliminary considerations are extensive. Eight of the twelve chapters in the book are in fact concerned with philosophy per se; three-fourths of the total number of pages thus deal with principal philosophical issues which must be considered prior to the discussion of Nygren's own approach to philosophy of religion and theology. With this well-planned and carefully executed analysis of philosophical foundations, Nygren has not only recaptured his position as the most advanced methodologian in the Lundensian tradition; he has also established himself as a major contributor to the philosophical debate in the third third of the twentieth century. His views must now be reckoned with wherever philosophers consider what philosophy is.

In the present chapter we shall seek to summarize Nygren's approach to certain basic philosophical issues as this has now been fully formulated.[2] Our purpose is to sketch in outline the profile of a figure whose features now more than ever have become clearly marked and who stands among contemporary philosophers as an authority of irenic proportions. We shall need to keep our sketch sketchy, obviously, and remember that our interest here is simply to describe how one of the makers of the modern theological mind has sought to find a proper philosophical base for what we might call a scientifically respectable approach to philosophy of religion and to theology, in the present and for the foreseeable future. And we must keep our description descriptive, holding criticisms to a minimum and reserving constructive alternatives for a later occasion.

TOWARD A SCIENTIFIC PHILOSOPHY

Philosophy, as Nygren sees it, comes in two principal forms, one metaphysical and the other scientific. This has been so from the beginning, even though the forms of metaphysics have changed from time to time, as has the nature of science. Philosophy was born under the double stars of religion and science; it came into being with a bifocal orientation—toward the universal as well as the particular. Ingrained in the very essence of philosophy are thus two equally important, equally valid concerns. Yet there is tension between them—a tension which threatens to destroy the unity of the philosophical perspective. The history of philosophy is in fact the story of how the two elements of the philosophical orientation have fallen apart and have been pursued, one at the expense of the other.

According to Nygren, the origin of metaphysics as a separate discipline came with Aristotle. Yet it was Aristotle who also introduced into philosophy the very factor which was eventually to spell the end of metaphysics. Incorporated in the structure of Aristotle's thought—besides the superstructure of universal concerns and metaphysical perspectives—was an entire substructure of particular or empirical interests, the rudiments of a scientific point of view. At this early stage in the history of Western thought, the two could coexist more or less harmoniously as occupying separate stories in the philosophical building; but, in Nygren's terminology, Aristotle had built into his structure "an explosive" which, in time, was bound to go off. With the development of the empirically oriented sciences in modern times, the explosion came, resulting in a complete bifurcation between science and metaphysics and a total separation of the original bifocality of philosophy—the concerns for universality and particularity. Particularity became the domain of the sciences; universality, the concern of philosophy, i.e., metaphysics.

Nygren's analysis of the development of philosophy under the impact of the modern sciences is quite instructive. He does not enter the conflict on one side or another, playing one kind of thought against the other, but asks instead to what extent a philosophy constituted either as metaphysics or as science can do justice to both of the original foci of philosophy—the particular and the universal, observations and principles.

The metaphysical tradition in philosophy, as Nygren describes it, went through a hardening process as the scientific disciplines rose to challenge the authority of philosophy in field after field. Left finally without a claim in the empirical realm altogether, philosophy retreated to a realm where the particular or special sciences had no standing at all—the realm of absolutes, of ultimate realities, of being itself. There it proceeded to develop its ontology (the science of being as such), its axiology (the theory of the transcendent unity of being and value), its world view (the interpretation of existence as a whole), and its system (the complete, all-inclusive, integrated and unified structure of all reality and all knowledge), partly by way of a fundamental methodological assumption, conceptual realism (the idea that concepts, ideas and values are representative of real objects, transcendent substances, things in themselves), and partly by way of two basic logical procedures, deduction and induction. In metaphysics, then, the universal interests of philosophy were nurtured to the fullest.

But the scientific interests? Nygren recognizes, of course, that metaphysics also makes claims to be science, but it is obviously not scientific in the same sense as the special sciences. Faced with the criteria of science that have been generally accepted among the empirical sciences—which is where, after all, we have finally learned what real science is—metaphysics has been forced to either scale down its scientific claims, and claim to be something else, or to inflate its claims, and claim that what it is is indeed science. In either case, however, the scientific character of metaphysics is in question. Metaphysical ontology, for example, is not scientific in any acceptable sense of the word. Had metaphysics simply investigated *what we mean* when we say that something *is*, it could have been. But it goes on in its conceptual realism—off the deep end, as Nygren judges it—asking about "being in general," "being itself," "true reality," "the ultimate nature of existence," or the like, and such questions are not, strictly speaking, scientific. They are, in fact, meaningless, since there is no possibility of finding the right answers—no possibility of finding answers at all. And the same is the case with the other characteristics of metaphysical thought; such a philosophy falls short of the scientific standards on every count. The equation of being and value obviates objectivity. The orientation on a certain world view is clearly subjective and arbitrary, despite all claims to being true or absolute. Conceptual realism builds on the illegitimate assumption that the particular is identical with the universal. And the metaphysical use of deduction and induction is fraught with arbitrary assumptions and logical circularity. In sum, whatever else metaphysics may be said to be, science it is not.

We should note that Nygren does not find metaphysics an altogether invalid intellectual enterprise. To distinguish it from science is not to rob it of all significance and all meaning. The error of metaphysics is not that it is not scientific, but that it claims—unjustifiably—that it is. Nygren can in fact speak positively of the role of metaphysics in terms of "conceptual poetry"—as poetry, not science. Unacceptable as it is when regarded as a science, metaphysics gains new significance and new freedom when considered as a branch of art. Even though it must be robbed of any scientific pretensions, it can in fact make important contributions to science—as intuition, viewpoint for detecting connections, discovering clues, suggesting hypotheses, and the like.[3]

But if metaphysics is discredited as a science, what options are left for the philosopher who desires to be scientific? Two, says Nygren. He can either model his philosophy on the special sciences, or he can structure it independently in the form of a scientific approach to universals. The first option has been tried in a variety of ways, with philosophers anchoring their discipline in the sciences of psychology, mathematics, and semantics—but always with disastrous results. The role of philosophy in the empirical field has become increasingly tight. Psychology, for example, has developed more and more into an experimental science, leaving little room for specifically philosophical procedures. Mathematics and logic are, of course, closely related, and this makes possible a certain cooperation between them. But only a limited number of philosophical problems admit of solution via strict mathematical models. And a philosophy that is defined in purely linguistic categories has always had problems justifying its existence in distinction from the science of semantics. As Nygren describes the situation, the attempts to establish philosophy on the model of the special sciences are consistently being wrecked on one of two cliffs: any attempt to identify an empirical subject matter that is unique for philosophy is always frustrated by the fact that the special sciences have already occupied all conceivable areas of study; and even if it should succeed, philosophy would thereby only have established itself as a special science, not as philosophy. Moreover, if it were to go this way, philosophy would inevitably fall into the trap of adopting a particular point of view and treating it as though it were a general philosophical standpoint—which is metaphysics, the very thing which philosophy must avoid if it is to be scientific in the first place.

For Nygren, then, the only option which remains is to define philosophy properly as a universal science. This means that the scientific nature of philosophy is to be affirmed, but that it is directed, not toward particulars, but toward universals. Philosophy does not have a special area of its own but is involved in every area, raising questions that are of fundamental importance to all areas of knowledge or science. Its unique task is to identify the universal presuppositions which are implicit in human experience and human awareness of any kind, and it goes about its work by way of methods and procedures that are as recognizably scientific as those that are employed by the empirical sciences.

This is the philosophy which Nygren goes on to delimit and describe as follows.

FORMS OF SCIENTIFIC ARGUMENTATION

When he comes, first, to the problem of defining the scientific nature of the universal science, Nygren is immediately aware of the need for an exact criterion of what constitutes a "science." He raises the issue in terms of three principal questions: (1) What is it that characterizes a scientific procedure? (2) How far does philosophy possess the requisite qualifications for this? (3) What is the difference between scientific philosophy and other sciences?

Nygren's answer to the first question is simple in form but of principal significance: What characterizes scientific procedure is "the possibility of objective argumentation."[4] As Nygren defines it, argumentation means "giving reasons for and against a proposition or idea put forward by oneself or somebody else"; objective refers to what Nygren describes as "testability," "intersubjectivity," and "reproduceability"; and possibility functions to soften somewhat the outer limits of science while at the same time drawing the line against those kinds of activities that are not "possibly" scientific—though not for that reason illegitimate or insignificant. In choosing to focus on "the possibility of objective argumentation," Nygren has at the same time dismissed a series of other conceptions of what is characteristic of science—"a common deposit of truths," "the progressive certainty of science," "the scientific method," and the like. As Nygren sees it, the first of these conceptions is static, while science is dynamic; the second is presumptuous, while science —when it is truly scientific—is humble; and the third is quite simply a myth—science has not only one method, it has many. The character of science is not determined by its material, its methods, or its results, but by the nature of scientific procedure.

With his definition stating that scientific procedure is characterized by the possibility of objective argumentation, Nygren has formulated a principle which is capable of application both in the sciences and in the humanities. The basic procedure is the same, even though the methods may vary. For example, the natural scientist and the historian are one in regard to scientific procedure; they both propose certain hypotheses which they proceed to test with reference to the material they study, and in objective ways. But their methods of study and testing are different, as is their material. At times, various disciplines may share their methods or utilize each other's methods in interdisciplinary or transdisciplinary ways. What makes such cooperation possible is the fact that all the disciplines of scientific study are based on the same fundamental principle: the possibility of objective argumentation. Normally, however, the disciplines of study develop methods that are particularly appropriate to their own material or objects of study; what makes these separate methods legitimate from a scientific point of view is the fact that all scientific study is related to a single procedural principle: the possibility of objective argumentation.

But does philosophy—the science of universals—have a form of objective argumentation? And is it unique? To answer these questions, Nygren looks first at the main forms of argumentation which the sciences have come to employ, testing whether they are at all applicable to the specific tasks of scientific philosophy. Basic to Nygren's considerations here is a historical inquiry focusing on the origins of those perspectives which now govern the scientific mind.

Nygren finds these perspectives going back to Gottfried von Leibnitz and David Hume, and particularly to Leibnitz's theory of truth. Leibnitz distinguished between two kinds of truths—eternal or necessary truths (truths of reason) on the one hand, and contingent or dependent truths (truths of fact) on the other. The first were said to be true in any and all circumstances; the second, only in particular cases, as the circumstances happen to be.

Leibnitz's perspectives were of course such that they allowed free play both to rationalistic and empiricistic approaches to truth, but as Nygren looks at it, the separation of truth into two kinds of truths put both science and philosophy on the wrong track. Nygren puts it this way: "The trouble starts—quite innocently—with *substantivization*, goes on through the addition of the definite article and the use of the plural form to *substantialization*, and ends in a metaphysical fog." [5] Moreover, by setting necessary and contingent truths over against each other, Leibnitz exposed both philosophy and science to the double temptation of *judging* one kind of truth by another or *reducing* all truth to one or the other kind. Both rationalism and empiricism have in fact shown a propensity to fall for this temptation. Leibnitz and Hume are themselves "good" examples of the tendency to reduce all truth to the standard of one (in Leibnitz's case, eternal truths, in Hume's case, generalizations from observation) and to judge one kind of truth by the criterion of another.

To Nygren's way of looking at it, all of this is nonsense—"a metaphysical fog." There are no eternal or necessary truths;

what has been called so is nothing but logical consequence, based on hypothetical assumptions and developed by way of syllogistic argumentation. Neither are there any so-called contingent truths; what has been called so is simply what is or is not the case in a certain situation and what is true—and cannot be otherwise—even if the situation is ever so contingent. Says Nygren:

> If what is meant by the formula "necessary and contingent truths" were the whole truth about "truth" it would mean that there was no truth at all. It would be the ruination of the very idea of truth, and the inevitable result would be scepticism.[6]

That skepticism is indeed the inevitable result of Leibnitz's perspectives is demonstrated, says Nygren, by what has happened both in rationalism and empiricism. Rationalism seeks to obtain certain and indubitable knowledge by basing everything on a given set of axioms, but it has not been able to give convincing reasons for the validity of the axioms themselves. Empiricism seeks to obtain clear and verifiable knowledge by going back to the bedrock of human experience, but it has always had difficulty getting beyond the level of sense impressions. Both perspectives are thus fraught with skepticism, even though they both fight against it, one by way of idealistic metaphysics, the other by way of sensualistic solipsism.

In Nygren's view, what is really involved in the differentiation between rationalism and empiricism is not two kinds of truths but two different modes of scientific argumentation—the axiomatic mode and the empirical mode. In analyzing these, Nygren hopes to find what it is that characterizes basic scientific procedure—the criteria by which even scientific philosophy must be guided.

Axiomatic argumentation, as Nygren describes it, starts with a number of definitions, to which are appended certain axioms of unquestioned validity, and moves by way of a series of logical deductions (syllogisms) to the formulation of certain propositions that are already implicit in the original definitions.

Axiomatic argumentation is thus structured on a strict "if—then" model. It is clearly an objective form of argumentation; its conclusions are subject to proofs (logical proofs); and its results can be inspected and tested by way of an objective standard (logical consistency)—and all in the public view (intersubjectively).

Empirical argumentation is less unequivocal. As usually conceived, it starts with what is observed (the empirically given facts) and moves by way of induction and abstraction to the formulation of certain conclusions—certain principles (natural laws) which are seen to underlie the regularity of phenomena. Nygren does not accept this description of the empirical mode of argumentation, however. It makes induction into a mirror image of deduction—simply an alternate form of logical inference—and this is not how the empirical sciences work at all. In actual practice, one finds that the relationship between observation and theory is almost the reverse. The scientist does not start with indiscriminate observations or a mass or atomistic data, but with an idea—what Michael Polanyi calls a hunch—which is crystallized into a hypothesis and subsequently tested by reference to the empirical material. Moreover, the results of the process are never, strictly speaking, "conclusions"; they do not have the proof value of strict logical inference, and they are never final. They remain tentative, hypothetical, more or less verified, but always open to further testing, and always liable to falsification.[7] As Nygren describes it, then, empirical argumentation is structured on the hypothesis-deduction-experimentation model, and contains not an if-then type of inference but a since-therefore relationship between hypotheses and facts. It is the dynamic interplay between theory and empirical material that gives empirical argumentation its unique character. And its scientific qualities are assured whenever the process is marked by objectivity, intersubjectivity, verifiability, and reproducibility.

From this analysis of the axiomatic and the empirical modes of scientific argumentation Nygren derives the standard by which every scientific discipline, including philosophy—the universal science—must be guided: "the demand for objectivity in argumentation, for intersubjectivity and openness for inspection, for the possibility of critically testing it and its results, and for whatever else belongs to scientific procedure."[8] In regard to philosophy, specifically, Nygren considers it imperative that its form of argumentation, whatever it is, be (1) equal to the other modes of objective argumentation, i.e., equally strict, equally predictable, equally consistent, and equally testable; and (2) distinct from the other major modes of argumentation, directed as it must be to the universal concerns which are the unique domain of philosophy.

But is there such a mode of argumentation? Nygren thinks there is, and he proceeds to show where and how it has developed. It is a distinctly modern development, though it has been hinted at at certain points in the past.

PHILOSOPHY AS ANALYSIS OF MEANING

The developments that have taken place in philosophy during the last half-century are extremely important, to Nygren's way of thinking. What has transpired is nothing less than revolutionary. A profound change has come upon the discipline, both in its self-understanding and in its procedures. The old philosophical systems are gone. The traditional interests of philosophers are set aside. What concerns philosophers in the modern age is the analysis of meaning, and what constitutes the primary focus of philosophy is language, the basic medium of meaning.

The new philosophy is not, of course, uniform; it comes in three kinds—existentialism, logical empiricism (or logical positivism), and linguistic philosophy (or language analysis). Nygren examines each of these at length, asking several probing questions that relate to his inquiry concerning philosophical argumentation: What is their relation to metaphysics? Do they achieve significant clarification of the scientific task of philosophy? How far do they succeed in distinguishing the function of philosophy from that of the special sciences, and thus in developing an authentic and independent form of objective argumentation for philosophy?[9] The criterion by which these philosophies are evaluated is thus the same one which has been central to Nygren all along: philosophy as the science of universals, without metaphysics. Nygren does not consider this an arbitrary criterion, imposed on philosophy from without; it lies, rather, deep in the nature of philosophical science itself. And measured by this basic standard, the three branches of modern philosophy appear, in Nygren's view, somewhat uneven.

Existentialism, as Nygren understands it, is probably the one modern philosophy that stands closest to the older philosophical traditions. It raises the age-old questions of essence and existence, being and nothing, etc., and continues—at least in its religious or Christian forms—to seek the meaning of life under the star of religion, of man in confrontation with God, of time in confrontation with eternity. Yet it has the appearance of being a modern philosophy. It shares with the others a basic aversion to metaphysics, a definite concern for meaning, and a strict phenomenological stance. As Nygren analyzes existentialism more closely, however, he finds that its analysis of meaning falls short of the scientific standard. Its approach to analysis is not characterized by objective argumentation but by intuitive perception; and its results are not verifiable, testable, and intersubjective, but solipsistic, capricious, and subjective. As regards scientific philosophical procedure, therefore, it can make no significant contribution; its significance is that of "conceptual poetry"—of metaphysics, not science.

Much more central to the modern breakthrough, says Nygren, are the various forms of logical analysis developed in the twentieth century—in England, by G. E. Moore, Bertrand Russell, and the early Ludwig Wittgenstein; in Sweden, by Phalén and Hägerström; and on the Continent, by the so-called Vienna Circle. They all share a vigorously antimetaphysical attitude, and they are all involved in the logical clarification of language—though in different ways. Moore worked on the basis of ordinary, common-sense principles, while Russell sought to construct a new, more exact, "ideal" language for philosophy.

The Uppsala philosophers sought to expose the logical contradictions of metaphysical thought, while the Vienna Circle attempted to develop a positive logical verification principle by which the actual truth-value of propositions could be determined.

But have these antimetaphysical philosophers themselves managed to avoid metaphysics? Nygren thinks not altogether. The logical positivists of Vienna are liable to criticism because of their positivistic ontology; they have also found themselves in trouble with—of all things—a verification principle that is not itself verifiable! Hägerström and his followers, by their constant appeal to the concept of reality, can also be seen to have allowed logic to slide into dependence on a positivistic ontology. And Russell's logicism—his development of an exact symbolic apparatus for purposes of formal logical analysis—has obviously not been a sufficient guarantee against the possibility of metaphysical excesses. Instead of clarification of the meaning of language, which is the announced objective of logical analysis, one finds evidence in every camp of the old fallacy of reductionism—the tendency, as Herbert Feigl describes it, "to cut with Occam's razor far into the flesh of knowledge instead of merely shaving off the metaphysical whiskers." [10] Such reductionism, in Nygren's view, is an inherently metaphysical tendency—the absolutization of a single perspective or a particular concept of reality.

It is the third of the modern trends, called language analysis or linguistic philosophy, which according to Nygren has exemplified the purest, most consistently scientific approach to the analysis of meaning. This is the philosophy of the later Wittgenstein and certain British linguistic analysts, among them Gilbert Ryle and John Austin. Here the philosophical enterprise is focused simply and solely on the clarification of the meaning of language. Metaphysical interests are laid aside; analysis is all there is to philosophy.

One problem with language analysis, in Nygren's view, is that its purposes—its aims or directions—have at times been left rather vague. The clarification of the meaning of language, if it is not given direction or purpose, may have difficulty proving itself scientifically important and philosophically relevant. Wittgenstein and Ryle do say that language analysis is directed toward philosophical problems, but what problems are to be considered is not specified. Austin is even less direct; in his view, language analysis—the clarification of language—is significant as an end in itself. In both cases the scientific purposefulness and philosophical importance of linguistic analysis seem to be put in jeopardy.

It is at this point that Nygren wants to go a step further and develop an analytical philosophy which is clearly directed toward the universal concerns of philosophy, but without metaphysics, and which is unquestionably scientific both in regard to its object of study and with reference to its mode of argumentation. He defines it simply as "analysis of presuppositions" or, in more explicit language, "logical analysis of the presuppositions of meaningful language." Every term in the definition is important. This philosophy is analysis, not metaphysics; it is analysis of meaning, not ontological speculation; it focuses on language, but is concerned with the basic presuppositions of meaning; it is clarification, but not reduction; it works by way of logical procedures, but steers clear of logicism. In it are gathered all the best tendencies from the modern analytical philosophies, and it has the potential for meeting all the basic criteria for a scientific philosophy which Nygren has placed before us. It is a universal science, not one of the special sciences. It has its own mode of argumentation, distinct from both the axiomatic and the empirical modes, one that is particularly appropriate to its own purposes. It is objective, open to tests, intersubjective. The analysis of presuppositions thus secures for philosophy the status of a universal science.

LOGICAL ANALYSIS OF PRESUPPOSITIONS

What precisely is the nature of the philosophical mode of argumentation?

Nygren dawdles a bit before describing it further. He wants

to indicate that his analysis of presuppositions is not an entirely new thing on the philosophical scene; it has parallels here and there in the work of other philosophers, past and present—in Phalén's conceptual analysis, in Wittgenstein's ideas concerning language games and rules of play, in Edmund Husserl's phenomenological analysis, as well as in the tradition concerned with validity and the transcendental a priori which goes back to Kant. Nygren considers, in fact, the concern for presuppositions of meaning equivalent to the concern for validity. In both cases it is the basic criterion of meaningfulness which is at stake; the presupposition for the validity of a statement is at the same time the presupposition for its making sense.

Nygren also wants to have his readers understand precisely what is meant by the concept "presupposition"—he spends an entire chapter, in fact, delimiting it from other, illegitimate interpretations. He distinguishes it first from prejudice, a judgment which is passed before (*prae*) the case has been brought to trial (*judicium*). Prejudices, says Nygren, are particular, material judgments that precede analysis; presuppositions are general, formal principles that are discovered as a result of analysis. Moreover, prejudices are subjective and arbitrary; presuppositions, objective and given—they are the ultimate, inescapable bases of all meaningful awareness or experience.

Nygren next distinguishes presuppositions from axioms and hypotheses. Axioms are initial assumptions that are considered self-evident and from which theorems and propositions are deduced by way of deductive reasoning; they are the starting point of axiomatic argumentation. Hypotheses, likewise, are the starting point of empirical argumentation—they are theories which are to be validated by reference to the empirical facts. Axioms are absolute; hypotheses tentative. Presuppositions, as defined by Nygren, are different from both. They are not the starting point of philosophical argumentation but the results. They are absolute, but not in an ontological sense, only in a logical sense; they are validated, but not by empirical evidence, only by being shown to be the ultimate and necessary bases of all meaningful experience, universally. Because presuppositions are different, philosophical argumentation is also different. It starts, not with absolute axioms or tentative hypotheses, but with meaningful experience and valid statements, seeking to work its way by analytical means back to the presuppositions of meaning and validity which are in fact at work.

In using such terms as *absolute, ultimate,* and *necessary* in connection with his definition of presuppositions, Nygren is aware that he has come close to the concept of "absolute presuppositions" with which the philosopher of history R. G. Collingwood works. There are, in fact, some similarities in the perspectives of Collingwood and Nygren. Collingwood's metaphysics is not directed toward ontology, but toward the absolute presuppositions which underlie the very structure of human thought—the way we ask our basic questions. This is Nygren's focus also. But Collingwood's analysis of presuppositions, his metaphysical analysis, focuses primarily on human consciousness and historical awareness, and this, in Nygren's view, is much too narrowly psychological and phenomenological. Nygren is committed to the principle of *logical* analysis—nothing else is worthy of the philosophical mode of argumentation. He is afraid that Collingwood's kind of presuppositions may turn out to be no more than the suppositions of certain individuals or groups of people—what Nygren identifies as fundamental motifs, and which are the objects of historical-systematic investigation, motif research, not strictly speaking *philosophical* analysis.

Several additional distinctions are drawn by Nygren in the interest of clarifying the concept of presuppositions, namely between logical presuppositions and preunderstanding, and between presuppositions and prescription. The first is in contrast to existentialist hermeneutics, particularly Rudolf Bultmann and Paul Tillich; the second, in contrast to Kant. The problem with existentialist hermeneutics is that it is interested in philosophical analysis only to the extent that it serves the purposes of theology; philosophy uncovers the questions, theology furnishes the answers. But the questions are not here open, formal, universal, or presuppositional; they are content-defined, material, specific, or prejudicial. Preunderstanding is therefore not the same as logical presuppositions. The problem with prescription is rather more complicated. As Nygren sees it, Kant is consistently preoccupied with epistemological subjectivism—with the spontaneity and activity of the subject in the process of knowing. For Kant, therefore, the presuppositions of understanding are the products of the understanding, prescribed by the knowing subject, and thus phenomenal, not given. Kant has namely been caught on the horns of the subject-object dilemma; he is anxious to avoid all traces of metaphysics, all objectivistic ontology, and he seeks refuge in phenomenology, treating existence as a world of phenomena which correspond to the laws or categories which the knowing subject prescribes. Nygren has no need to go in that direction; for him the subject-object dilemma is not a problem. Knowledge is always a dynamic interplay of subject and object. In his view, therefore, presuppositions are not *granted*, prescriptively, by the subject; they are *given*, presuppositionally, in the interaction between the knower and the known.

What are presuppositions, then? Nygren defines them as "logically necessary fundamental presuppositions." They are the presuppositions that are actually at work in all meaningful experience and language, and which we cannot avoid accepting and depending on if we are to maintain the judgments or statements which we make about the world or about our awareness of it. They are of such a fundamental nature that without them experience itself would not exist. They are basic to all thinking and speaking, determinative of the meaning we experience in experience. They are categorical in the sense of logical necessity, for they are implicit in every assertion we make, already affirmed in the utterance of any proposition.

With this Nygren is finally ready to outline the analytical processes with which the philosophical mode of argumentation operates. The method, basically, is Kant's. It is described by Kant as "the critical analysis of synthetic a priori judgments," or as "the transcendental deduction of a priori categories." Nygren prefers to call it simply "the logical analysis of presuppositions," but Kant's terminology is fully acceptable to him, if it is understood correctly. In identifying the method as "criticism," Kant has namely distinguished the analysis of presuppositions both from dogmatism and from skepticism—i.e., both from the postulation of arbitrary suppositions and from the denial of the presuppositions which our statements actually affirm. "Critical" analysis is directed to laying bare the presuppositions which we in fact take for granted in the various areas of our experience and thought. Kant's way of referring to the objects to be analyzed as "synthetic a priori judgments" is also, according to Nygren, a stroke of genius. Prior to this, the a priori categories had been considered axiomatic or tautological (analytic); in describing them as synthetic, Kant has indicated that philosophical analysis starts with experience and focuses on the presuppositional categories which are implied in experience. Critical philosophy is thus defined with explicit reference to scientific perspectives. Finally, in describing the analytical method as "transcendental deduction," Kant has indicated both that the process is a logical one and that it represents an attempt to work one's way back to the formal, universal—transcendental—presuppositions which are implied in experience. This is sound, says Nygren, but the terminology must be kept clear of traditional associations: deduction, in Kant's perspective, is not the syllogistic process which characterizes axiological argumentation; and transcendental, in the context of critical philosophy, does not have the metaphysical connotations which it carries among conceptual realists.

Presuppositional analysis, as Nygren outlines it and as Kant originally developed it, is a process that includes two distinct steps: (1) the analysis of concepts, and (2) the logical analysis of presuppositions. The first is a negative step, the second a positive. *Conceptual analysis* is simply the process of clearing away confusions and contradictions in the experiential material or in the propositional language with which the philosopher works. The aim is to make sure that the various dimensions of experience or contexts of meaning are not jumbled together in an indistinguishable mixture, but that each element of thought and each concept referred to represents a clear and distinct idea, and that each aspect of experience and each propositional statement is understood on the basis of its own presuppositions. When a consistent element of experience or a noncontradictory statement or proposition is thus identified, *the logical analysis of presuppositions* is undertaken in order to establish the principal presuppositions or presuppositional categories which lie behind the experience or which are implied in the utterance of the proposition. It is as simple as that.

Or is it? Nygren has not actually demonstrated how a specific instance of presuppositional analysis would work. He seems to assume that both conceptual analysis and presuppositional analysis are well known and established philosophical procedures. Moreover, he seems to assume that these procedures are by definition objective and scientific—as immune to subjectivism as they are to metaphysics. This may be somewhat optimistic on Nygren's part. In seeking to clarify the logical structure of philosophical analysis, for example, Nygren limits himself to referring to two familiar concepts of logic, namely, "implication" and "necessary and sufficient conditions." *Implication* is of course a rather loose term, so Nygren must qualify it by adding the adjective *strict*—"strict implication." Presuppositional analysis, as Nygren describes it, is "an attempt to discover what is logically implied in an empirical proposition which no one denies." [11] But how? The logic is "strict implication," "strict logical consequence." But is not all deduction, including that which characterizes axiological argumentation, based on strict implication? Yes, says Nygren, but it is here that the second element of logic, *the distinction between necessary and sufficient conditions*, comes in and serves to specify what characterizes the philosophical-analytical mode of argumentation. In philosophical analysis, the relation between a proposition and its presupposition is this: "the presupposition which is implied in the proposition is the *necessary* condition for the proposition, while the proposition is simply the *sufficient* condition for the presupposition." [12] The two are inseparably interlocked, but in such a way that while each is a condition for the other, they are so, in a manner of speaking, in directly opposite ways. The relationship between presupposition and proposition—the structure of their logical implication—is thus entirely different from that which exists in axiomatic argumentation between an axiom and the theorems which are derived from it.

Nygren has not taken the clarification of basic philosophical procedures any further than this. If we are still anxious to see how the analysis of presuppositions actually works, the only option is to take the principles and apply them to a specific case. Nygren's own interest in engaging himself in the discussion of the nature of philosophy, and in trying to develop the philosophical mode of argumentation, has been to lay the basis for a scientific approach to philosophy of religion. We should therefore be able to see how Nygren applies the scientific principles developed here when we come, next, to consider his views on that subject.

IV. Analytic Philosophy of Religion

Anders Nygren's philosophical interests have never been purely theoretical. He is aware that philosophy can never be significant if it is pursued without reference to the actual experience of human beings. As the universal science, philosophy is not removed from man's existential concerns; on the contrary, it is related to every field of human knowledge and thought.

The particular field of experience and thought with which Nygren is primarily concerned is religion. His extensive inquiries into the nature of philosophy are clearly undertaken for the purpose of laying the foundations for philosophy of religion and theology—and in such a way as to secure for these disciplines a place among the sciences of man.

Nygren first approached these concerns in the early 1920s in the context of Kantian criticism and Hägerströmian positivism. Positivism was the negative factor in the situation, criticism the positive. On the negative side, Nygren found it impossible to go against the antimetaphysical emphases of the leading Swedish philosophers at the time—he decided to avoid metaphysics like the plague. It was the first requirement of any philosophy of religion and theology which desired recognition as a science. On the positive side, Nygren found a useful philosophical perspective and a possible scientific procedure for philosophy in Kant. His own inquiries were thus oriented to the leading issues of philosophical criticism—criteria of validity, a priori categories, transcendental analysis, and the like. In regard to philosophy of religion, however, Nygren was forced to go beyond Kant. Kant had subsumed religion or religious awareness under the category of ethics. Nygren, on the other hand, was anxious to understand the essential nature of religious awareness and distinguish it from other categories of experience, both so as to avoid confusion in the relationship between religion and other categories of experience and so as to interpret religious awareness in terms of its own unique character. And in this connection Nygren found the perspectives of Friedrich Schleiermacher more helpful.

When Nygren returned to the field of philosophy and resumed his inquiries into philosophy of religion fifty years later, the situation was different. Philosophy had changed. No longer was he confronted with Kantian issues and positivistic restrictions. A new philosophy had developed, one which was more open to the particular concerns of the philosopher of religion and more advanced in regard to scientific philosophical procedures. The age of analytical philosophy had dawned and, as we have seen, Nygren found himself at home in it. Not only were many of his earlier perspectives confirmed and broadened in the thought of contemporary philosophers, but Nygren actually discovered that philosophy of religion fits naturally in the larger framework of analytical philosophy and needs no longer to defend itself against opponents who either exclude religion from consideration altogether or reduce it to some other, more acceptable, form of human awareness. In this situation, Nygren found it a good thing to be a philosopher of religion again.

In the present chapter we shall look at Nygren's approach to the philosophy of religion as this has now been formulated with reference to the contemporary situation in philosophy. We shall follow his own presentation in *Meaning and Method* rather closely, not adding other references to his earlier works than those Nygren himself makes. By this procedure the reader will be able to observe Nygren's thought in its most relevant form and grasp the significant developments in Nygren's perspectives without having to struggle with earlier terminologies and philosophical issues that are no longer up to date.[1]

MEANING AND CONTEXT

When Nygren defines the scientific task of philosophy as the "logical analysis of presuppositions," he has presented the most elemental definition he can think of—and also the most general. He never forgets, however, that the presuppositions philosophy is after are the presuppositions of validity or sense or meaning, and that the analysis of presuppositions is simply a description of the scientific approach to the analysis of meaning. It is in the question of meaning—the meaning of meaning—that all the lines of Nygren's philosophical investigations converge; and it is from the basic consideration of the presuppositions of meaning that both his philosophy of religion and his theological methodology emerge. At the transition between Nygren's philosophy and his philosophy of religion stands his theory of meaning, and it is to this we must now devote some paragraphs.

Basic to Nygren's theory of meaning is the close relationship which exists between meaning and context. Nygren gives an entire chapter of *Meaning and Method* to this point, once more emphasizing the close affinity between his own views and those that have come to the forefront among analytical philosophers in the twentieth century. What has happened in analytical philosophy is described as a transition from atomism to contextualism.[2]

The roots of the analytical theory of meaning go back, says Nygren, to Gottlob Frege's famous distinction between *Sinn* (sense meaning) and *Bedeutung* (reference meaning).[3] Frege was a mathematician and a semantic analyst in whose thought were anticipated many of the most characteristic emphases of analytic philosophy—the differentiation between reference and meaning, ordinary speech and technical language, words and sentences, contexts of meaning, and much else. Most interesting in Frege's thought, as Nygren looks at it, is his view that *words* have *reference* while *sentences* have *meaning*. In this lies the seed both of logical atomism and the linguistic-analytical identification of context and meaning.

Nygren notes that there is nothing in Frege's view of the reference value or signifying function of words which requires the development of an elaborate ontology of language. Words can be considered simply as signs whose function is to signify or refer to something. The so-called problem of how a sign can signify or represent an object is not, in Nygren's view, a real problem. Like the old epistemological question of how subjective human consciousness can claim to go outside itself and grasp the objective world by way of cognition, it is a pseudo-problem. It is in the nature of consciousness to be conscious of something; it is likewise in the nature of a word that it refers to something. Frege, however, did not seem satisfied with that. He compromised the original clarity of his thought, first by giving sentences both a sense and a reference value, and secondly by attaching to his general theory of signs or names an ontological, even metaphysical reference to "that"—i.e., an objectified entity—which the name names. This was all part of Frege's attempt to build an ideal language and give thinking the quality of an exact logical-mathematical calculus, and this same combination of semantic metaphysics and symbolic logic is evident, says Nygren, in many of Frege's followers—most especially Bertrand Russell.

Russell can be said to be Frege's counterpart in the twentieth century—both positively and negatively. He was so, positively, in seeking to work out the symbolic structure and the logico-mathematical principles of Frege's ideal language; and he was so, negatively, in denying Frege's link between meaning and context and substituting the exact opposite affirmation, logical atomism. Russell's negative relationship to Frege included even the rejection of the distinction between sense and reference. In Russell's view, it was all the same, namely, denotation. There is no meaning beyond reference. Significance—which is all there is left of meaning—is simply a matter of signification, and it is gotten at simply by breaking sentences down into their component words and complex words into their atomistic particles.

If Nygren regrets what happened to Frege's theory of meaning in Russell's atomism, he applauds the reversal of Russell's approach initiated in the later works of Wittgenstein.[4] Here the trend was once more turned in the direction of meaning and context. Having started out as a follower of Russell, Wittgenstein little by little discovered the restrictions and limitations of the picture theory of language. He discovered that the words we use are not limited to a single signification; they are capable of being used in any number of language games, each with a different set of rules, each with a unique sense or meaning. As an illustration of the revolution which took place in Wittgenstein's philosophy of language, Nygren refers to the change he underwent in regard to ambiguity. In his early period, Wittgenstein had considered ambiguity a defect in ordinary language—something which was to be removed by restoring language to an exact logical standard. Later, ambiguity was no longer a defect but evidence of the capacity of words to be used in a multiplicity of language games and contexts of meaning. Ambiguity is therefore not a problem, only a pseudoproblem. It can be overcome simply by examining the rules of the game that is being played, the use to which words are put in the particular context. As Wittgenstein says, "It is the particular *use* of a word only which gives the word its meaning.[5]

To Nygren, this reversal in Wittgenstein's view of ambiguity is symbolic of the antithesis between the atomistic philosophy of Russell and the contextual theory of meaning of linguistic analysis. Russell had said, "Sentences are composed of words, and have meaning derivative from that of the words that they contain."[6] In contrast, Wittgenstein suggested that "only the sentence has sense; only in the context of a sentence does a name have meaning."[7] With the later Wittgenstein, the influence of logical atomism was broken and Frege's original distinction between reference and meaning was restored. Meaning is now clearly a function of context. And with this Nygren is well satisfied—contexts of meaning have in fact been the key to his own theory of meaning all along.

CONTEXTS OF MEANING

Nygren's theory of meaning is essentially a theory of contexts, but contexts not merely in terms of sentences and paragraphs—the "immediate context," as he calls it—but rather in terms of a comprehensive set of basic categories or presuppositions which serve as a framework of meaning for language or as a total context of meaning within which experience is experienced as meaningful. Nygren prefers to call them "contexts of meaning," since various alternative descriptions such as universe of discourse, frames of reference, standpoints, perspectives, areas of experience (Nygren's earlier terminology), and language games (Wittgenstein's phrase) all prove to have certain unfortunate associations—metaphysical, ontological, subjective, atomistic, or arbitrary. His aim is to avoid all such nonscientific tendencies while yet distinguishing between various fundamental dimensions of experience and language. In choosing to call them contexts of meaning he is clearly in line with the earlier analysis of presuppositions. It is these fundamental principles—"the logically necessary fundamental presuppositions"—that govern and give coherence to the various basic contexts of meaning; without them, neither experience nor language would be meaningful or valid.

Two points are important to Nygren in regard to the contexts of meaning: their multiplicity and their ultimate integration. The first is a fact of life which analytic philosophy cannot ignore; the second is a philosophical goal which the universal science cannot disregard. Philosophy must assume the double responsibility of clarifying the difference between various basic contexts of meaning and showing exactly what is the relation between them. It must analyze each particular context of meaning in terms of its autonomy and integrity; and it must hold them all together within a comprehensive "context of contexts" and demonstrate how they are integrated within a unifying framework of meaning. The work of philosophy is not done until both of these tasks have been accomplished.

We must note that Nygren's own emphasis throughout his career has been on the autonomy of the separate contexts of meaning. He has never managed to develop an overall, inclusive, integrated system of presuppositions.[8] The closest he comes to a comprehensive view of "the context of contexts" is in the essay, "The Permanent Element in Christianity," in a section entitled "The Life of the Spirit." [9] Here Nygren outlines a series of "great questions" or "indispensable concerns" which have emerged in more or less stereotyped forms wherever spiritual life exists or whenever the enduring cultural institutions of society are established. These are, first, "the question of truth" (institutionalized in science); second, "the question of good and evil, right and wrong" (institutionalized in law and ethical traditions); third, "the question of the beautiful or the sublime" (institutionalized in art); and fourth, "the question of the eternal" (institutionalized in religion).

In *Meaning and Method*, Nygren refers to the same four contexts of meaning, but he does not consider them a closed system. He concentrates on identifying those contexts of meaning which are *given* in man's experience and which we encounter in the form of historical realities—science, morality, art, religion—or in the form of fundamental human questions—the true, the good, the beautiful, the eternal. In principle, the basic contexts of meaning are "a small number of comprehensive viewpoints or ways of looking at things which have gradually crystallized in the course of history." [10] We do not ourselves create them; philosophy does not invent them; they are there before the philosopher begins to do anything about them; we confront them simply as a matter of experience. They are the basic, historically given "forms of life." [11] But there is no guarantee that this particular list is exhaustive. The system is never closed. The philosopher must always be open to the possibility of new contexts emerging. Nygren indicates, in fact, that there may be reason now to consider economics and technology such independent and autonomous contexts of meaning.

In emphasizing the autonomy of the different contexts of meaning, Nygren desires to avoid two elementary metaphysical errors, namely, the absolutization of a single context and the confusion of contexts, or category-mixing. Absolutization, whether on the part of science or on the part of religion, is altogether illegitimate from a logical point of view. It forces material that belongs to one context of meaning or that answers to a different presuppositional question into conformity with a particular set of presuppositions or a context of meaning which is considered normative. Such dogmatism is not only simplistic —it is logically corrupt. And so is category-mixing. The confusion of contexts, the uncritical jumping of fences or shifting to and fro between different presuppositional frameworks, not respecting the autonomy of any of them, leads to the loss of understanding, first of the meaning intended, and ultimately of all meaning whatever. The process is by definition reductionistic, and its result is inevitably disorientation, meaninglessness, nonsense.

According to Nygren it is precisely in its role as the universal science that philosophy must assume responsibility for keeping order among the contexts of meaning or serving as a clearing house for the presuppositions underlying the entire system of meaning. But its task is analytic, not metaphysical. Nygren stresses that no preconceived theory of meaning can determine what is to be regarded as a genuine context of meaning or decide what the final shape of the total system of meaning might be. It is in the presuppositions which govern each individual context that the laws are laid down for the interpretation of experience and the understanding of language:

> Science must be understood scientifically; otherwise it loses its scientific meaning.
>
> Ethics must be understood ethically; otherwise it loses its ethical meaning.

> Aesthetics must be understood aesthetically; otherwise it loses its aesthetic meaning.
>
> Religion must be understood religiously; otherwise it loses its religious meaning.[12]

These and other autonomous contexts of meaning must be respected for what they are; the phenomena of human existence must be approached without prejudice. The analytical philosopher takes a broad perspective and is universal in his interests. He analyzes the characteristic content of each dimension of experience and seeks to identify the fundamental presuppositions which are determinative of their uniqueness and integrity. And the same approach must be followed in regard to the systematic integration of the contexts of meaning as well. The analytic philosopher does not impose a preconceived system; he analyzes the interrelationships between the various fundamental forms of life, seeking to discover the principle which underlies the complementarity of these many contexts of meaning within the totality of human life. As Nygren sees it, the separate presuppositions are joined together by some sort of "presupposition of presuppositions." [13] It is this ultimate presupposition—the fundamental principle of all meaning and understanding whatever—that philosophy, the universal science, must ultimately seek to find. And it is by way of the analytical method, not by way of metaphysics, that it must proceed. The scientific approach to the presupposition of presuppositions is none other than the logical analysis of presuppositions.

THE RELIGIOUS CONTEXT OF MEANING

If philosophy in general is the analysis of contexts of meaning, philosophy of religion is the philosophical analysis of the religious context of meaning. Says Nygren, "The philosophy of religion is the logical analysis of the fundamental presuppositions in the area of religion." [14] This is Nygren's definition of the discipline and the sum total of his elaborate endeavors to lay the foundations for a scientific approach to it. Nygren has not—

as we have already observed—gone very far in the actual work of presuppositional analysis, generally, or in the direction of a transcendental deduction of the religious category, specifically. *Meaning and Method* has been restricted to questions of prolegomena, and Nygren has not in any other connection shown us how "the logical analysis of the fundamental presuppositions in the area of religion" is done. But he has said some important things about the religious context of meaning and about religious language, and it is these aspects of his philosophy of religion that we shall take note of here.

Of primary importance is Nygren's emphasis on the empirical grounding of philosophy of religion. Basic to the scientific analysis of any context of meaning is, as we have seen, to take account of the phenomena that are given in man's experience and history. The scientific approach to philosophy of religion is likewise based on sound knowledge of the facts, specifically of the phenomena of religion, of the givens within the religious context of meaning. The material in which the presuppositional analysis is to be grounded is not created by the philosopher of religion; it is there in the form of actual religious experiences and events, on the contemporary scene or in the historical record. The philosopher of religion must therefore be an informed observer—perhaps even a participant—of religious life. The more inclusive and objective is his knowledge, the better able he will be to undertake the presuppositional analysis in a responsible scientific manner.

Nygren has here opened up the possibility of relating philosophy of religion to a number of other disciplines which study religious phenomena from a variety of perspectives—the history of religions, religious anthropology, sociology of religion, psychology of religion, textual criticism, theology, and liturgics, to name only the most obvious. The discipline has thus been given an interdisciplinary starting point, and this is clearly in character with Nygren's definition of philosophy as a universal science. Philosophy of religion is that branch of the universal science which concerns itself with religious phenomena, universally.

But if philosophy of religion is thus related to the other sciences that are concerned with religious phenomena, it is of particular importance to Nygren to point out that the discipline also has a unique function—one that is related to its role as a universal science and which none of the special sciences of religion can fulfill, namely the analysis of the logical presuppositions that are foundational to the authentic meaning and autonomous significance of religious experience and religious language. In fulfilling this function, philosophy of religion gains status, not only as an *independent* science, but as the *principal* science in the the field of religion. And as such, it comes to have significance for the special sciences of religion as well. For until the question of the autonomous nature of the religious context of meaning is clarified by philosophy of religion, all kinds of "foreign" notions—metaphysical ideas, category mistakes, etc.—are likely to invade the religious context and be given free play in religious experience and in the study of religious phenomena. Theology, above all, needs to be made aware of this, for it has a tendency to broaden its perspectives and claim to represent, not merely religious meaning, but universal truth or essential knowledge—meaning that is relevant to all fields of knowledge and applicable to "natural man" as well. To Nygren's view, such broadening of the theological perspectives represents an absolutism and a confusion of basic contexts of meaning which is both untenable and illegitimate.

In regard to religious language and the interpretation of religious meaning, specifically, Nygren emphasizes that philosophy of religion functions to secure an understanding of religious statements which "lets religion be religious" [15] and to develop an interpretational principle (hermeneutics) which allows religion to speak for itself. Responsible interpretation must endeavor to get as close as possible to the original meaning of religious statements, texts, propositions, or messages—original, that is, both in a historical sense and in the theological, intentional, or categorical sense. Here the limits are set for hermeneutics. It is not the business of the interpreter to create or even re-create (reinterpret) the original message—only to interpret it in retrospect to its original meaning.[16] Says Nygren, "The content of a message is determined by the one who sends it, and the one who transmits it (the 'interpreter') has no business to remodel it to suit either his own or the recipient's ideas." [17] Moreover, the interpreter must not tear the message out of its own context of meaning. In Nygren's language, hermeneutics and contexts of meaning are so closely related as virtually to "coincide." It is precisely the context of meaning which determines what the message is all about. "Only that interpretation of a religious text or . . . phenomenon which sees these things in terms of their own religious context of meaning can give a correct account of their meaning—their own meaning." [18]

It is commonplace among modern interpreters of religion to point to the metaphorical, symbolic, or even paradoxical meaning of religious language. In Nygren's opinion, such generalizations say very little about the nature of religious meaning. What language does not employ symbols and metaphors? When psychology speaks of man's "inward" experience, it is not much different from the religious reference to God as "the most high." In either case, only a simpleton would be likely to be confused as to whether the spatial reference is literal or symbolic.

On the other hand, when the opponents of modern interpretations of religious language charge the proponents with reducing the Christian message to "mere symbols," "nothing but metaphors," "sheer contradictions," or other such negatives things, Nygren once more emphasizes that there is a basic lack of understanding of the unique nature of religious language at work. Whether one proposes or opposes a symbolic understanding of religious statements, one is in need of the kinds of clarifications which it is the unique function of philosophy of religion, in the form of logical analysis of the presuppositions of religious meaning, to give. Says Nygren, "If we wish to express something that belongs to one context of meaning in the language of another, we cannot do this by direct translation, but only by way of symbolic or metaphorical *periphrasis*, or by means of a parable."[19] To attempt to force religious language into an objectifying mold, away from its characteristic use of symbols and metaphors, is to restrict the linguistic tools of religion drastically and to force religion into metaphysics—and metaphysics both in the sense of category mixing and in the sense of conceptual realism.

Religious paradoxes are an area of religious language which is in need of basic clarification, both among the proponents of paradoxality and among its opponents. Nygren thinks the philosophical analysis of contexts of meaning can make a special contribution here. Paradoxes, when they appear in the normal course of logic or science, are of course contradictions—signs that something has been thought wrong, contrary to the rules of logical argumentation or without respect for the conventions concerning scientific evidence. As such they must clearly be removed. But a religious paradox is not a contradiction. It could be better termed a "transdiction"—an attempt to express some meaning that is part of religious awareness in terms that are borrowed from another language context. A religious paradox is a warning of the fact that there is something unusual going on in religious language, that there are aspects of meaning that can only be expressed in dialectical ways, and that there are contrasting truths involved which must not be avoided. A religious paradox is in fact an invitation to interpret what is said within its own particular and extraordinary context of meaning, and not by reference to criteria that are alien to it.

THE CATEGORY PROBLEM

When Nygren in *Meaning and Method* finally arrives at the point where he can no longer postpone the crucial question, "What exactly are the presuppositions which govern the religious context of meaning?" he is aware that he is faced with a problem. It is much easier, he says, to discuss negatively the disastrous consequences of not recognizing the particular categories that are appropriate to the religious context of meaning than it is to demonstrate positively what these categories are.[20]

The problem, in part, is that a regular definition of the actual content of the principal presuppositions or categories of religion is not possible; all we can hope to do is to analyze what is in fact presupposed when we make a religious utterance or state a proposition of religious import. But even this, says Nygren, is extremely difficult. For one thing, there is such a multitude of different, even contradictory and mutually exclusive religious statements around. Moreover, since religion is the most personal and commitmental of all realities, it is difficult to be entirely objective and comprehensive about it. However, Nygren desires at least to show how the land lies or to indicate, "at least sketchily," the direction in which a solution is to be sought.[21]

Without actually undertaking the procedures which he has defined as the appropriate method for logical analysis of presuppositions, Nygren suggests that "the category of the eternal" is still the most suitable terminology for describing the basic presupposition of the religious context of meaning. What commends this particular concept is that it, more than any other concept he can think of, meets the requirements which he has determined to be necessary if any such presuppositional category is to be philosophically acceptable, namely, that it can serve to indicate the *distinctive* character of the religious context of meaning—i.e., the integrity of religious awareness—and point the way to the ultimate *integration* of the various contexts of meaning within a single, wholistic system of meaning. Says Nygren, "Take away the perspective of eternity, and religion disappears . . . ; take account of the perspective of eternity, and you have a vast context of meaning which can do justice to the actually given religions and provide the key to a meaningful religious language." [22]

Nygren feels, however, that he must qualify the concept of eternity somewhat. As a religious category it must be understood as involving personal engagement or existential decision and is not to be identified with the abstract and impersonal concept of eternity which is typical of metaphysics or speculative philosophy. Eternity, when understood religiously, has significance for life. It has a bearing on the here and now. It has to do with the deepest issues of our existence, with the intersections between time and eternity which take place within concrete experiences of life in the world—experiences of revelation, judgment, reconciliation, and fellowship with God.[23] Eternity is not a time above time or an extension of time backwards or forwards, but a breakthrough in time. As Nygren says in another context, "The necessary conditions for religion are lacking unless this present world of sense is set over against the world of eternity, and unless this life of ours is viewed *sub specie aeternitatis*, in the light of eternity. . . . It represents a life which knows that it is not subject merely to the conditions of finitude."[24]

There is one final point which must be considered here, namely, Nygren's emphasis on the formality and openness of the religious category. One reason that Nygren has come to focus on the eternal as the preferable formulation of the basic presupposition of religious experience is that it involves absolutely no preconceptions in regard to content. As a categorical question, it does not prescribe what the answer should be; it allows every religion to work out its own particular answer.

This, of course, is fully consistent with Nygren's principal analysis of the nature of presuppositions. As we have seen, presuppositions are not to be content-defined, normative concepts which determine what is or is not an acceptable or valid experiential content. Such conceptual realism is utterly illegitimate within a philosophy which is structured as a universal science. Analytical philosophy of religion is not in the business of defining an ultimate criterion by which actual religions are to be judged but only to identify the formal presupposition on the basis of which they are to be understood. Philosophy of religion does not even claim to have identified the essence of religion—that irreduceable core which is "religion itself," "universal religion," "natural religion," or whatever else one might call it. It simply analyzes the historical religions for the purpose of penetrating to that fundamental presuppositional form into which they have all poured their particular content. There is no religious entity that corresponds to the presuppositional form;

all there is are the religions of the world. These are the essence of religion, each in its own way. Different in content, they are one in one thing; they express the way men and women have experienced themselves in time confronted with the eternal.

We shall not take this any further here—we have already encroached on the subject of the next chapter. Only this must be added: Anders Nygren's philosophy of religion, incomplete and unfinished as it is, not only points the way to an objective, scientific approach to the discipline. It also shows us how, by way of scientific procedures, we can come to the point where the religions of the world can both be recognized in their individuality and affirmed in their validity as representing different species of a single, unified genus.

V. Religion, Religions and Christianity

One of the characteristics of twentieth-century theology is a distinct and broadly dispersed aversion to the concept "religion." In the tradition which is identified as neoorthodoxy, and in its counterpart on the other side of the theological spectrum, liberal humanism, *religion* has come to be an odious word. Both camps have in fact desired to speak in terms of "religionless Christianity," although in actual use the phrase has come to mean different things to different people.

Neoorthodoxy sets religion in dialectical contrast to revelation. The first represents a God-relationship which originates as a human quest or as an upward thrust of worship or works which is formalized or structured in a variety of institutional procedures. The second describes a God-relationship which is characterized by divine initiative, by a downward movement of grace which is received by man in the context of an existential religious commitment. Christianity, says neoorthodoxy, is not religion; it is revelation. The religions of the world are not revelation; they are the attempts of man to establish a God-relationship on his own terms, by his own efforts.

Liberal humanism agrees with one aspect of the neoorthodox view, namely its anti-institutionalism, but only to say that religion—the institutionalization of faith—makes objective and static a dimension of man's life which is instead subjective and dynamic. Here the contrast is between faith and religious institution, or between spirit (or life) and letter (or doctrine).

Anders Nygren has no such hang-ups over the term *religion.* It is a perfectly useful concept and does not necessarily contain the odious implications which have been given it by the theologians of our time. A simple conceptual analysis would in fact show that both neoorthodoxy and liberalism have first loaded the term with certain theological or psychological preconceptions, then confronted it with their own particular prejudices, and finally dismissed it altogether as useless.

As Nygren understands the term, it refers quite simply to that dimension of human experience which has to do with religious meaning—however this is conceived or whichever form it might happen to take. It is, in a sense, an empty category. It does not predefine what religion *is,* only what it *does.* It does not determine what is the *content* of religion, only the *presuppositional context* of religious meaning. Christianity, Judaism, Islam, Hinduism, Buddhism, Shinto—they are all manifestations of religion, regardless of how they otherwise define themselves individually.

RELIGION AND THE RELIGIONS

As we have seen, Nygren is eager to emphasize that philosophy of religion is not in the business of developing a normative concept of religion, only to analyze the logical presuppositions which underlie the various conceptions of religious meaning which men do have. The philosopher's interest is not to identify the essence of religion, but only to clarify the essentiality of religion within the experience and awareness of man. "Religion," singular, is an abstraction; the reality of religion is to be found in "religions," plural—in the multiplicity of religious forms which have emerged on the human scene and throughout history.

But what exactly is the relationship of the one and the many, between religion and the religions?

This question is of fundamental importance to Nygren. It bears on the central issue that has concerned him throughout, namely, the establishment of a scientific approach both to philosophy of religion and to theology. But it has relevance also to issues that are more practical and immediate in the contemporary religious situation. Religious pluralism is a fact of life that has become increasingly troublesome as men of different backgrounds and different religious traditions have come closer to one another, within local communities, in states and nations, and on the international scene—in the global society of men. There is no denying that religion comes in many forms, and that these religions are fundamentally different—at times even contradictory. It is impossible to avoid the impression, also, that all religion, in whatever form, makes claim to absolute validity and in fact has such absolute validity for individual followers and groups of believers. Is there any basis at all for unity between the religions? Do they have anything in common? Is there a possibility for interreligious dialogue? For mutual recognition?

Nygren's approach to philosophy of religion opens up a way to deal with such questions in an objective, nondogmatic way. To understand it, we shall need to take one more look at certain aspects of Nygren's principal investigations of philosophical procedure.

As we have seen, the maxim under which Nygren explains the relationship between presuppositional categories and empirical-historical realities is that of questions and answers. The logical presuppositions function as so many formal, fundamental questions; the experiential material represents a series of material, content-defined answers.[1] But the matter is really not that simple. There is a two-way relationship in effect between questions and answers, a mutual interdependence of formal presuppositions and material facts. On the one hand, the questions or presuppositions are derived by way of logical analysis of actual phenomena or experiential contexts of meaning; they are anchored in the empirical-historical realities of human life and not imposed on the material in any arbitrary or prejudicial manner. This is what we might call the *logical* relationship; it is evident in the analytical move from experience to presuppositions. On the other hand, the various questions or formal presuppositions, once they are identified, are placed in direct contact with the factual material within the appropriate contexts of meaning, and this material is subsequently interpreted in the light of the respective presuppositional questions. This is what we might call the *hermeneutical* relationship; it is manifested in the interpretive move from presuppositional questions to experiential answers. Nygren takes the first, the logical relationship, to be the particular province of philosophy, the universal science; the second, the hermeneutical relationship, is the responsibility of the special sciences in each field of study. In the context of religion, the first is assigned as the special responsibility of philosophy of religion; the second is distributed among the various disciplines of theology.[2]

At this point, however, another complication comes into view. As Nygren analyzes the relationship between formal presuppositions and empirical content, he discovers that this relationship varies between the different contexts of meaning. Particularly significant is the difference between the way this relationship is structured in the context of science and the way it functions in the contexts of ethics, art, and religion. In science—the theoretical contexts—the connection between fundamental presuppositions and empirical material is more or less direct. Men have reached a certain consensus as to what constitutes objective scientific procedure. There are conventions and rules, formal and informal, which are recognized throughout the scientific community. Although the methods vary from discipline to discipline, the basic idea of what constitutes science and scientific procedure is the same throughout. In ethics, art and religion—the three atheoretical contexts—on the other hand, no such consensus exists. All sorts of subjective or commitmental standpoints are at work, and these introduce an element of discontinuity within the empirical-historical material related to these fields—a separation between persons and groups on the basis of their different ideas as to what exactly is the appropriate understanding of the good, the beautiful, or the eternal. In the context of ethics, there are a number of conflicting traditions of morality, each with a different idea of the good as the organizing principle or basic motif. In the aesthetic context, likewise, there are a number of schools of thought, different conceptions of style, and so on. And in the context of religion there are perhaps more differences of opinion and more fundamental divisions of standpoints than in any other context. Here are in evidence the different world religions, the many major traditions within each, numerous confessional subgroups under these, and in addition an infinite variety of doctrinal schools and theological persuasions, all based on a different idea as to what the experience of the eternal is all about.

Thus, while in the context of science the historical-empirical material can all be studied within a single framework of meaning, namely, on the basis of the logical presuppositions which apply to science as a whole, in the context of religion two separate presuppositional frameworks or contexts of interpretation must be considered: one primary, that of the religious context of meaning as a whole, and one secondary, that of the particular motif context or ideological tradition within which the material in question belongs. The first, as we have seen, is the special concern of philosophy of religion; the second is the primary responsibility of the theological sciences.

We shall not consider in detail Nygren's delineations of the science of motif research at this point—it will be the subject of a following chapter. What we do wish to point to here is that in making these distinctions, first between a primary and a secondary context of meaning, or between a category context and a motif context, and second between philosophy of religion, the analysis of formal presuppositions, and theology, the study of material presuppositions, Nygren has in fact given us the key to the solution of the problem of the one and the many. In the perspective of the first and primary context—the category context—or on the basis of the formal logical presupposition of religion, all the religions of the world are *one*. In the perspective of the second or secondary context—the motif context—or on the basis of the particular ideas which are presuppositional for individual religions, they are *many*. Philosophy of religion, functioning in the form of presuppositional analysis, provides the perspective within which all the religions of the world can discover their *unity*. Theology, functioning in the form of motif research, provides the means by which each individual religion can be understood in terms of its own *integrity*. Here, then, is the basis for dialogue between religions: on the one hand an objective, historical-analytical approach to the philosophy of religion; on the other hand an objective, historical-analytical approach to the study of theology. In the first context, dialogue is based on a general presuppositional category which is the common presupposition of all religious meaning; in the second context, dialogue is based on the open recognition of the particular motifs that are formative of the individuality or unique character of each religious type.

THE NATURE OF RELIGION

One may desire to ask at this point whether Nygren's objective, logical-analytical approach to philosophy of religion is in fact capable of serving as basis for interreligious dialogue. Does it not aim to define religion simply in terms of an open and empty category—a form into which anyone at any time may pour any content whatever? What is there to guarantee that the dialogue on religion will actually be a dialogue between religions? And what is there to guarantee that when religions talk about religion, they have in fact something in common to talk about? Are we not, as Sigfrid von Engeström, one of Nygren's critics, once commented, "at a loss to say whether one who has a positive religious faith of some sort is thereby more legitimately committed to the category of the eternal than one who only believes in the multiplication table?" [3]

Nygren has two answers to such questions. The first is that the formal presuppositional category, although an abstraction, is not derived by way of abstraction.[4] The basic presupposition underlying the religious context of meaning is the result of a logical analysis of the given historical-empirical phenomena of religion.[5] The second is that the formal presuppositional category, although open and empty, is not formless. The presupposition that underlies religious meaning may not say anything about the *essence* of religion, but it may still say something about the *nature* of religion. When the presuppositional category, which is silent by itself, is held together with the historical-empirical material—the actual phenomena of religion—the category of eternity takes on certain existential qualities which can be observed as the characteristics of religious experience or religious meaning, wherever it appears. Eternity may not by itself specify what is the nature of religion, but "the existential experience of an encounter with the eternal" does. As Nygren says:

> The investigation of the [religious] *a priori* has demonstrated what we might call the "place" of religion within [man's] consciousness. Then follows the question whether this place is "empty" or filled with concrete reality. This question cannot be answered through philosophical speculation, but only by taking it to experience. There religion meets us in a multitude of psychological and historical facts; that is where the religious *a priori* is realized.[6]

Thus, in response to the half-facetious remark by von Engeström, one might say that while in principle the concept of the eternal includes both those who have a positive religious faith and those who believe in the multiplication table, in practice the experience of the multiplication table—the existential relationship to it—is vastly different from the experience of the eternal or the existential consciousness of being confronted by eternity.

How then does the experience of the eternal shape up? What are its characteristics? What is the actual nature of religion?

Nygren's answer is a beautiful exposition of the existential qualities of religious experience.[7] Wherever religion occurs, it is characterized by four specific encounters with the eternal: (a) it is experienced as the *unveiling* of the eternal; (b) it is experienced as the ultimately serious, disquieting *judgment* of the eternal; (c) it is experienced as the positive resolution of the human predicament, as *reconciliation* with the eternal; and (d) it is experienced as a vital, fulfilling relationship, *fellowship* with the eternal. Each of these experiential characteristics of religion are of course interpreted differently within the different religions, but as Nygren sees it, the basic structure of religious experience is the same throughout.

The reference to "the unveiling of the eternal" points to the *revelational* quality of all real religion. As Nygren explains it, there is no religion that does not contain this sense of encounter with the eternal. Particular religions may not speak of it in terms of a confrontation with God—there are religions that lack any God-concept. But no religion limits itself to the world of sense, to mere facts or finite realities. The religious consciousness is the consciousness of an encounter with the eternal, the ineffable, the infinite. Within or without, whether in the interior of the soul or in the cosmos of spirit, it is an experience of mystery, an overwhelming awareness of "otherness." Yet it is always concretized, always related to the actualities of life. The eternal is encountered in the finite; the ineffable in the perceptible. That is why, in the history of religion, revelation has always been identified with such concrete symbols as fetishes, images, and incarnations. The locus of revelation may vary from religion to religion, but revelation has always a locus of some sort.

The reference to "the serious, disquieting judgment of the eternal" points to the *radicality* or *gravity* of all real religion. Nygren finds this manifested at all levels of religious experience—from the primitive conceptions of *tabu* to the higher consciousness of the *holy*. In the confrontation with the eternal, man is aware that he stands in the presence of the ultimate, the powerful, the pure. And in this encounter he is shaken, judged, challenged. The experience of the eternal begets a disquietude of spirit, a sense of crisis, a radical transvaluation of all values. It gives man a consciousness of responsibility, of unconditional answerability, of sin and guilt. The eternal casts its light on the worldly, and the secular stands unworthy before the sacred. The concept of sin may differ in the different religions, but all religions do have a conception of sin.

The third characteristic of the experience of the eternal, "the positive resolution of human unworthiness," points to the *soteriological* (saving) quality of all real religion. Nygren has no hesitation on this point. All religion contains the idea of salvation or provides a way to overcome the tension between revelation and judgment, between the eternal and the sinner. A religion which did not make possible a reconciliation between the eternal and the unholy or which did not undertake to bridge the gulf it has created would be a monstrosity. The ideas differ, of course. There are soteriologies which are focused on man's own purification—on rites, observances, or works which the sinner must perform in order to acquire the qualities of the eternal. And there are soteriologies which focus on purification which proceeds from the eternal—on an atonement which is God's own work and which is offered man as a gift of grace. It is perhaps possible to argue that the latter is the more sensible idea. To require of man, who is already deep in the crisis of judgment, that he must work his way out of his own crisis is in some ways a contradiction in terms. But regardless of such differences in views, a view of salvation is present in all religions.

The fourth and final feature of religious experience, "the vital, fulfilling relationship with the eternal," points to the *relational* or *communal* quality of all real religion. Nygren takes this to be a universal orientation within the most diverse forms of religion, from the primitive idea of union by eating with—in some cases actually consuming—the deity (as in the totemistic sacrament) to the mystic's purely spiritual absorption into unity with the eternal. All religion aims ultimately to bring about fellowship between the eternal and the temporal, between the divine and the human. With the initial alienation of the two overcome, a new relationship of complete openness and mutual indwelling is established. The divine life permeates the human; finite man finds his fulfillment in the eternal. The structure of the relationship may vary from religion to religion, but a relationship there is in all religions.

TYPES OF RELIGION

Nygren's analysis of the characteristic qualities of all genuine religion does what it is designed to do—it gives empirical or existential shape to the formal presuppositional category of the eternal. It provides at the same time a philosophical basis for interreligious dialogue, or even an agenda for such conversations, one that outlines what the various religions—as types of religion—are all about, yet without ignoring the existence of certain individual differences and without disregarding the distinct motif structures which are characteristic of each.

But a dialogue between religions on the basis of a general outline of the existential qualities of religion—i.e., on the basis of an objective, analytical philosophy of religion—touches only one aspect of the relationship between the one and the many. The other aspect must also be in the picture, namely, the autonomy, the integrity, even the absoluteness which typifies the individual motif structures and the different religions. Interreligious dialogue must, if it is to be honest, take account of the *theological* differences between religions and find a way to bring these into view, both so as to allow full recognition of the individuality and authenticity of each religion and so as not to allow any one viewpoint to be absolutized beyond the relative absoluteness which it has in relation to the motif context within which it belongs.

The problem of interreligious dialogue requires, in other words, that both philosophical and theological perspectives be included. But in order to avoid confusion and subsequent misunderstanding, or even breakdown in conversations, the two perspectives must be kept from running over into one another. It is clear, on the one hand, that the *philosophical* perspective, which focuses on the analysis of religion in terms of a general presuppositional category, leaves no room for absolutist claims. Here the relativity of religious types is a fact of life. The various religious types, while acknowledging their differences, analyze their way to the presuppositional category of religion or to those universal qualities of religious experience which are basic to the empirical nature of religion. The *theological* perspective, on the other hand, is oriented to the explication of the particular motif contexts of individual religions, and it represents therefore a narrower perspective. Here the religious commitments which are typical of individual religions are basic. Everything is seen from the viewpoint of such commitments, and they are acknowledged as absolute, at least in the view of those who hold them. There is no relativity in the perspective of a believer; only one view is possible.[8]

One should think that this reference to the absoluteness of individual religions or different motif contexts would be the end of interreligious dialogue. Not so, for Nygren. The theologies which emerge on the basis of particular motif commitments may also be studied in an objective, scientific and intersubjective manner—on their own, and in comparison with one another. This is the function of motif research. Built on the foundations of philosophical criticism, and structured as a scientific discipline of historical-systematic analysis, motif research assumes responsibility for the investigation of the basic motif structures which are characteristic of each individual religion. It analyzes these motif structures in isolation from other motif structures, seeking to clarify the distinct ideas or essential nature of each individual type. And it sets the different motif structures in comparison with one another, seeking to find out how they are related to one another and how they differ from each other. Motif research is thus a procedure which is capable of holding together both the relative absoluteness of individual theologies and the absolute relativity of theological standpoints. If the analytical philosophy of religion is the clearing house between major religious types, motif research may well be said to be the way the ground is cleared for theological dialogue across commitmental lines.

We should note that Nygren has not himself done the kind of

structural analysis of different motif contexts which is necessary as basis for a full-fledged interreligious dialogue. He has limited himself to hinting at the multiplicity of motif structures while analyzing only two major types, namely, the egocentric and the theocentric, or certain eros-oriented and certain agape-oriented motif structures.[9] In the context of ethics he has applied generally the same typological principles, setting over against one another various moralistic or legalistic ethics, on the one hand, and the attitudinal or spontaneous ethics on the other.[10] In all these investigations, Nygren has been preoccupied with the contrast between Christianity and Platonism or—what for Nygren amounts to the same—between the evangelical Christian understanding of the gospel and the neoplatonic, Roman Catholic, and liberal humanistic interpretations of Christian faith. He has been anxious, of course, to point out that the dialectical contrast between egocentricity and theocentricity is nothing more than a working hypothesis and does not imply any value judgment. He has also been eager to emphasize that the sharp over-againstness which he sets up in the relationship between Christianity and Platonism is simply an analytical procedure, for purposes of typological comparison and motif clarification, not an attempt to prove the superiority of the Christian perspective. One must take Nygren's own word as regards his intentions. But the effect of the particular working hypothesis which Nygren applies has nevertheless been to give his readers the impression, not simply of typological investigation and typological comparison—which is motif research pure and simple—but of typological purism and typological advocacy. And that, one must admit, is not an adequate basis for sound, open, and authentic dialogue between types of religion or types of theology.[11]

But if Nygren's own motif research has tended toward typological purism and typological advocacy, and shows the effects of using the dialectical contrast between egocentricity and theocentricity as a filter for sifting a variety of historical-empirical materials, particularly the motif contexts of Christianity and Platonism, this in no way diminishes the value of motif research as a theological method or as a possible basis for objective, intersubjective, scientifically responsible dialogue between religious types or across commitmental lines. There are indications, in fact, that when Nygren's method is freed of Nygren's own primary working hypothesis it becomes a very valuable tool for basic research in a variety of fields.[12] The exploration of the possible contributions of motif research in the context of interreligious dialogue has also begun.[13] We shall look more closely at the method itself in chapter VIII.

CHRISTIANITY AS RELIGIOUS TYPE

Returning now to the main purpose of our analysis here, we shall look finally at Nygren's principal approach to the determination of the essential nature of Christianity—Christianity as religious type—namely, that which is based on his philosophy of religion. We have already observed how Nygren has sought to clarify the nature of religion by specifying the existential qualities or experiential structure of the encounter with the eternal—the revelation of the eternal, the judgment of the eternal, the reconciliation with the eternal, and the fellowship with the eternal. These, to Nygren, are the characteristics of all religion, all types of religion.

But what of Christianity? Does it fall within the same spectrum? Says Nygren, exactly so! Individual religious types are not distinguished from others by the addition or subtraction of certain elements of religious experience—i.e., by formulating a spectrum of existential encounters with the eternal which functions as the unique property of this one religion—but rather by the unique way in which they, each one, interpret the various facets of religious experience which are fundamental to the nature of all religion. In a crucial statement of procedure, Nygren defines his approach as follows:

> If one desires to come to a scientific conception of the essential nature of Christianity, . . . one must begin with the "place" of religion within [the] spiritual life [of man], as this comes to

> expression in the transcendental presuppositional category, and on that basis determine in what sorts of "moments" [or facets] of experience this religious category is realized in all religion. Since by this procedure the nature of religion is in one sense disclosed, the inevitable background for the [determination of the] nature of Christianity is also given. The essential nature of Christianity can from this perspective not mean anything else than the individual *gestalt* [structure] which these same experiences, [characteristic of] the nature of religion, assume in Christianity.[14]

This is precisely the procedure which Nygren follows in his book *Det bestående i kristendomen* (included as "The Permanent Element in Christianity" in *Essence of Christianity*). Here, following an opening section entitled "The Life of the Spirit" in which he identifies the place of the religious question among the fundamental questions man asks in life, Nygren includes a section entitled "Religion," in which he explicates the essential nature of religious experience in terms of the four moments of existential encounter with the eternal which we have outlined above. Then in a third section entitled "Christianity," Nygren raises the question of the particular gestalt or unique structure which marks these same existential moments in Christianity.

We shall not consider the details of Nygren's explication of the essential nature of Christianity here—it is the subject of chapter IX. Our interest in this context is principally to identify the procedure and to analyze Nygren's philosophical approach. In this connection, two particular points are important, not only to our understanding of Nygren's general perspectives on philosophy of religion but also to the development of a sensible approach to interreligious dialogue. They are, first, that Nygren *considers Christianity one among the many religions of man,* and second, that Nygren *takes full account of the essentially Christocentric character of Christian faith.* Nygren's perspectives include, in other words, both the relativity of Christianity and the absoluteness of the Christian faith, and it is this fact which makes Nygren's approach particularly relevant to the issues of interreligious dialogue.

As we indicated a moment ago, interreligious dialogue must be established on the basis of two fundamental assumptions: that all religions are in some sense one, and that the religions of man, though one, are in actual practice many. Dialogue must take into account both the unity of all religion and the diversity of separate religions, both the absolute relativity of religious types and the relative absoluteness of each individual type.[15]

On the surface, then, the dialogical endeavor seems paradoxical—and thus doomed to frustration and eventual failure. But that is so only if one fails to observe how the dialogical perspective is constituted. It encompasses two essentially different interests—one philosophical, the other theological. The *philosophical* interest is focused on the general concept of religion, universal religion; the *theological* interest has as its focus the individual types of religion, particular religions. In the philosophical perspective, religions are relative, and all religion is one; in the theological perspective, each religion is considered absolute and the religions of man many.

Thus Nygren's two emphases can both be seen to make sense. From the philosophical perspective, Christianity is one among the many religions of man and therefore a relative form of religion; from the theological perspective, Christianity is that religion which is characterized by the affirmation that Christ is the unique and ultimate manifestation of the eternal, and therefore—to the Christian believer—absolute.[16] It may be a little difficult to hold these two perspectives *together without confusion,* and *differentiated without separation.* The formula sounds like a Chalcedonian paradox—and for those who can think only in one framework of meaning at a time it may all be manifest nonsense. But Nygren persists. With appropriate clarifications, even a Chalcedonian paradox such as this can be made to make sense. In a statement that can easily be applied to the point at issue, Nygren says:

> The relation between the contexts of meaning is an illustration of the fact that there is nothing at all contradictory or paradoxical here. The individual context of meaning [in our case,

> the particular motif structure of a single religion] must preserve its complete distinctiveness and not be confused with other contexts [other motif structures], for such a confusion—such category mixing—inevitably results in a change and distortion of meaning, if not in complete meaninglessness. On the other hand, the individual context must not be isolated, it must not be detached from its indivisible and inseparable connection through presuppositions with the rest of the contexts of meaning [in our case, with the analysis of the nature of religion in general], for that would result in disintegration and annihilation of the context [or loss of dialogical basis].[17]

From Nygren's point of view, then, interreligious dialogue is a matter of respecting the theological integrity of each individual religion while at the same time seeking the philosophical integration of all religion. In entering into such dialogue, Christianity is called upon both to be true to its own individuality—to the absoluteness of its Christocentric commitments—and to be willing to recognize its empirical relativity and its place within the spectrum of universal human religion. That is the challenge. For those who have two eyes, or who have the capability of looking at things both philosophically and theologically, the two perspectives will work together to form a picture that has depth and meaning. For those who have only a single eye, or whose perspective is restricted to either philosophical or theological considerations, the picture makes no sense at all, and the whole endeavor is meaningless. And for those who do not see with either eye, or whose awareness of both philosophical and theological perspectives is altogether absent, even the suggestion that there is something interesting and useful in such explorations is ridiculous.

One can only hope that there will always be men like Nygren among us, to remind us that we do in fact have two eyes and that in looking at ourselves and others, singularly or in relation to each other, we should use both.

Part Three

IN SEARCH OF AN APPROPRIATE METHOD

VI. Theology and Scientific Methodology

Anders Nygren the philosopher is in service of Anders Nygren the theologian. It was in the interest of theology that Nygren originally became involved in basic philosophical investigations and in philosophy of religion. When he decided to explore the possibility of a scientific approach to the analysis of human experience, of the presuppositions of validity and meaning, and expecially of the religious context of meaning, it was—to quote the title of one of his early works—in order to lay "the scientific foundations of dogmatics."

Nygren's desire to establish theology, and especially dogmatics or systematic theology, as a scientific discipline of study was clearly related to the general situation of the discipline at the time—the general cultural context—as well as to the nature of theology or the character of the discipline as it had developed over the years. As Nygren saw it, the situation of theology in the modern age is really rather tight. Once the reigning queen of the sciences, theology has had to bear the indignities of a series of revolutionary attacks, first by the intellectual republicanism of the Enlightenment, and then by the scientific democracy of modern empiricism. In the process, theology was first dethroned, then exiled from the scientific community altogether. And the difficulties of theology in the politics of culture have obviously played back on the self-consciousness of theologians and the definition of the discipline as well. As refugees from science, theologians either went abroad, traveling about as dispossessed reactionaries making preposterous claims to continued intellectual supremacy, or into seclusion, perpetuating the old order in some secure cloister far from the maddening world of change. In either case, whether as unrealistic fools or as isolated dreamers, theologians seemed entirely out of touch with the mainstream of modern culture.

For Nygren, as a theologian, both the general situation of theology and the particular self-understanding of theologians were intolerable. Theology was in a sad state of affairs, and he decided to do something about it. He wanted to show that although the politics of knowledge has changed as a result of the scientific revolution, theology need not necessarily fall victim to the guillotine of criticism or suffer the sad fate of an expatriate of the old order; it can still exist and function within the new context. It can find a place in the new society, as one among the sciences of man, and not continue to prance about in the nostalgic exhibitionism of exiled royalty or isolate itself in the bitter world-negation of a defiant hermit. Theology, as Nygren came to see it, will never have any future in fighting against the scientific revolution; it will have to join in and prove itself capable of contributing to the new order in the world of knowledge. Theology will have to be redefined and reestablished as a scientific discipline of study. But for that to happen it will have to be willing to subscribe to the new constitution of science and approach its task on an equal basis with the other sciences of man.

It is in the interest of the democratization of theology, then, that Nygren undertakes to rethink the philosophical foundations of human knowledge. The scientific foundations of a new dogmatics must be built on the scientific approach to philosophy.

But with this, Nygren has clearly taken his farewell from various traditional conceptions of dogmatics. He has also, obviously, proposed an understanding of systematic theology which is at variance with several other major methodological alternatives in the twentieth century. To make clear how Nygren's methodology distinguishes itself from both traditional perspectives and other contemporary approaches to theology, we must first give some paragraphs to describing these perspectives a little more closely.[1]

DOGMATIC THEOLOGY

Traditionally, dogmatic theology[2] has taken one of two forms: it has either been a speculative or metaphysical endeavor, or it has been an ecclesiastical or confessional endeavor.[3] In the first form it has assumed the task of developing a system of universal truth, based on Christian assumptions but built by way of rational and logical procedures; in the second form it has taken responsibility for developing a system of particular truths, Christian dogmas, as these are understood by the Christian church as a whole or in a particular church community.

Both of these traditional forms of dogmatics have made claims to absoluteness; both have considered themselves normative disciplines, definitive of ultimate truth, though in different ways. *Metaphysical* dogmatics claims to represent the one, ultimate, and necessary framework of truth into which everything that is ever to be considered true must somehow be incorporated. Its claim to authority is founded partly on reason, partly on revelation, but the two are seen to coexist and cooperate harmoniously, mutually confirming and supplementing one another as two equivalent sources of knowledge. Church dogmatics or *confessional* dogmatics, on the other hand, is less presumptuous—or perhaps more—in that it claims to represent the transcendent truth that is revealed only to faith. Reason has no authority here apart from revelation. Revelation is the only source of truth, though reason can help in explicating it when it is directed by revelation and bound by the authority of revelation. Metaphysical dogmatics considers itself normative for all men; confessional dogmatics knows itself to be normative for those who share the true faith. Metaphysical dogmatics aims to make the truth known in such a way as to commend itself to all reasonable men; church dogmatics aims to present the truth as it was once delivered to the church and as it now confronts men in its own integrity, as a message of God and a challenge to men.

When Nygren considers both of these traditional forms of dogmatics unacceptable in the modern situation, it is not simply because *he* finds them so, but rather because the *situation itself* necessitates such a judgment. Nygren is not himself an iconoclast of theologies. He would have been perfectly happy to do theology in one of these traditional ways, if that had still been possible. But it is not. The modern age is a scientific age, and the scientific perspective questions the validity of all such theology, both because of the metaphysical character of speculative theology and because of the arbitrary character of confessional theology. Whether the claim to truth is universal and inclusive, as in the case of metaphysical dogmatics, or it is particular and exclusive, as in the case of church dogmatics, science puts it all to the same critical test—as it must. The test is namely not the test of science, arbitrarily imposed; but of man, of nature, of knowledge itself. Science has found itself forced to accept the natural conditions under which man exists, thinks, knows. It finds it impossible to accept any knowledge, any thought, which is not related to the actual conditions of man's existence. Science must quite simply challenge dogmatics to be as careful to observe the limits of reason as science itself is.

And Nygren accepts that challenge. He feels responsible for developing another approach to Christian dogmatics, one that can avoid the two features that cause the disqualification of traditional theology—metaphysical speculation and subjective arbitrariness—and one that is at home in the context of philosophical criticism and scientific empiricism.

When this is said, we understand at the same time why Nygren cannot subscribe to two major methodological alternatives which have been developed by other twentieth-century theologians, namely, the revelational church dogmatics of Karl

Barth and the correlational systematic theology of Paul Tillich. Barth's approach is too much like that of the world-estranged hermit; Tillich's bears too many of the characteristics of the presumptuous expatriate.

An interesting comparison between Barth, Tillich, and Nygren can be based simply on an examination of their relationship to philosophy.[4] Barth considers philosophy altogether extraneous to theology—as a perspective that has no bearing on the theological task at all. In fact, to anchor theological methodology in philosophy or base it on philosophical assumptions is to compromise the theocentric nature of theology and make it anthropocentric; it is to disregard the unique starting point which is given theology in revelation and to transform the Word of God into a "natural" human enterprise. So Barth must refuse any implication of theology with philosophy. Both theological method and theological content are based on revelation—i.e., on the assumptions that are internal to the Christian faith. Theology has a singular orientation on the Word of God; the Word asks the questions that are to be asked, and *it* provides the answers as well.

For Tillich the relationship of philosophy and theology is one of mutual correlation—an actual interaction of reason and revelation, culture and faith, the secular and the transcendent. Philosophy and theology deal with the same things, but from two different perspectives. The difference between them is not, however, categorical. Philosophical reason is in its essentiality the same as theological revelation, only that in its existentiality it is out of touch with its source. Reason is therefore confused, conflict-ridden, contradictory, until it is enlightened and reoriented by revelation. The correlation of philosophy and theology is characterized as a complementarity between something negative and something positive; philosophy can only ask the questions, while it is theology that provides the answers.

Nygren uses generally the same kind of language, as we have seen, but for him the complementarity between questions and answers means something entirely different. Philosophy and theology are considered two altogether different disciplines of thought, each with a distinct and significant function, but both related to the total theological enterprise. Each discipline has its own integrity, yet they are related to one another as two complementary sciences. Philosophy is the scientific inquiry into the principal presuppositions of experience and meaning—all experience and every kind of meaning, religion included. Theological methodology *must* therefore be anchored in philosophical inquiry; there is no way to avoid the anthropological grounding of theological method. The religious question is a human question, and philosophy is uniquely the analysis of human questions. But philosophy, the science of principles, does not provide the answers. They must be found in the actualities of experience—and religious answers in religious experience, in the motifs of faith and the structures of religious commitments and interpretations which it is the responsibility of theology, the science of religious motifs, to investigate. Philosophy is thus the analysis of questions; theology, the analysis of answers.

The comparison of Barth, Tillich, and Nygren not only reveals three fundamentally different understandings of the role of philosophy; it shows the three theologians holding three entirely different views of theology as well. Barth's approach is very much in the tradition of ecclesiastical-confessional dogmatics—Barth in fact entitled his major work *Church Dogmatics*. He is not in the business of developing a theology that will commend itself to men in general; he is bound by the authority of revelation to speak a word that comes from above and that is addressed to man but understandable only to those who are being grasped by it and who come to believe it. Barth's dogmatics is thus strictly an insider's theology, a norm of truth for men of faith, addressed to men outside simply by means of proclamation.

Tillich's, on the other hand, is a theology that is addressed to the world and designed to make sense as universal truth. It is a continuation of the speculative-metaphysical tradition—a *systematic theology* that includes both nature and the supernatural, the secular and the eternal, the finite and the infinite, in one grand synthetic unity. Tillich is not satisfied to speak to the believing few and in terms of revelational verticality; he considers the truths of faith truth itself—truth that will prove truthful even in the horizontality of reason. Tillich's systematics is thus an apologete's theology, presented as the universal norm of truth both essentially and existentially.

In Nygren's conception, theology cannot in the modern cultural situation be church dogmatics or apologetic systematics—such endeavors do not meet the test of science, i.e., the test of life, of logic, or of the human condition. There can be no science if the starting point is an exclusive set of assumptions or if the object of knowledge is transcendent to knowledge. Neither can there be science if the basis of thought includes both objective and subjective assumptions or if empirical and metaphysical procedures are mixed together. Nygren is bound to look for another option.

TOWARD A SCIENTIFIC THEOLOGY

If theology is to gain credence as a scientific discipline it is clear to Nygren that it must meet the requirements that are considered foundational in the scientific community. Philosophically, these are set forth in the epistemology of empiricism, particularly in the perspective of philosophical criticism. Practically, they are exhibited in the universal methodology of science or in the rules and conventions that are generally accepted among the sciences. The principal requirements are those which we have seen Nygren identify as objectivity, intersubjectivity, and testability. The practical requirements are (1) that a scientific discipline must have a given *subject matter*, (2) that every discipline of science must have an *interest* in this subject matter that is uniquely its own, and (3) that every discipline must have a *method* that is appropriate to its subject matter and purposes.[5]

It is in the light of these requirements that Nygren develops his definition of the science of Christian dogmatics or systematic theology. In general, he describes it as "the attempt that has arisen within Christendom to investigate Christianity in its historical beginnings and developments and by scientific means to understand the *egenart* [characteristic nature] of Christian faith and life."[6] More specifically, in Nygren's view, "the task of systematic theology cannot be other than to seek to understand and elucidate the Christian faith in its uniqueness, its distinctively Christian character . . . [and] its own inner organic coherence."[7] The definition is designed to show what the given subject matter of systematic theology is, what the theologian's unique interest is, and what the theological method must be. The *object* of study is Christianity, Christian faith and life; the theological *interest* is the characteristic nature of Christianity, its *egenart;* and the *method* is motif research. Thus, in every respect Nygren's conception of Christian dogmatics or systematic theology answers to the practical requirements of science, and when it comes to the principal requirements of objectivity, intersubjectivity, and testability, the discipline—as it is defined by Nygren—is fully capable of accreditation as well.

The details of Nygren's definition of the discipline will be analyzed in the chapters to follow. Chapter VII focuses on the subject matter of theology, chapter VIII on the method. Then, in chapters IX, X, and XI, we shall seek to follow Nygren's own way to the center of the Christian faith—to the permanent element, the central motif, and the key symbol of Christianity. The next several sections of this book are designed, in other words, to put flesh on the bones of Nygren's skeleton image of theology.

Before we proceed with the details, however, we must once more consider the two specific features in Nygren's approach that are determinative of his theological profile and of the way he develops his conception of scientific theology. They are related to the two principal traps that are lying in the way of scientific methodology for theology. Nygren has attempted to get beyond them by way of extensive analyses of the scientific approach to philosophy and philosophy of religion; he must now seek to steer clear of them in regard to the practicalities of theological methodology as well.

The first is Nygren's aversion to metaphysics. It has an effect on his views throughout—and here, in regard to theology, both on his conception of the theological subject matter, the theologian's interest, and theological method.

We have already observed how Nygren squares accounts with metaphysics on the theoretical level. From any scientific standpoint, metaphysics represents an illegitimate process of thought, and on two grounds: it ignores the limits of reason and steps beyond the boundaries of human knowledge, and it ignores the rules of reason and jumps across the fences between different contexts of meaning. In the area of theology, as in any other discipline of study, metaphysics represents both a presumption on reason and the confusion of reason, and all such distortions of reason must be checked by way of philosophical criticism. Thought must be held responsible to common sense and ordinary logic—or else left free to roam the universe in the form of conceptual poetry and intellectual playfulness without scientific pretense.

When Nygren comes to consider the question of the subject matter of theology in this light, he is required to observe two specific restrictions. First, the theologian cannot go beyond the bounds of experience. His object of study cannot be God, or eternity, or ultimate reality, for these are, strictly speaking, not objects of knowledge. He must have a subject matter that is given to knowledge, that is empirical in the ordinary sense of the term. Secondly, the theologian must not go beyond the bounds of religious experience or the religious context of meaning. Early in his career, Nygren spoke of this in terms of the religious "area of experience," and it sounded as if he wanted to limit the theologian within a very narrow range of experiences or to isolate theology from all the realities of life that are somehow outside the scope of religion. This is not, however, Nygren's intention. What he is after is not to limit the perspective of theology to religious realities, but to limit theology to the religious perspective on reality. The difference between the natural sciences and the religious mind is not that they deal with different realities, but that they deal with reality from different perspectives. Religion does not function legitimately as natural science, or as law, or as art; neither does science, or law, or art have a legitimate function as religion. Theology must therefore be oriented on the unique sense of meaning which characterizes the religious perspective; it must function on the basis of the critical awareness of the logical presuppositions which govern the religious context of meaning. It is for these reasons that Nygren defines the theological object of study as "faith"—faith as a historical-empirical reality, as the material realization of the formal category of religion—and in the case of Christian theology, specifically, *Christian* faith.

Second, in regard to the theologian's interest, Nygren's aversion to metaphysics once more affects his views. It brings him to look for a purpose for theology that is within the range of scientific possibility. And here again certain important restrictions are at work. The theologian cannot aim to construct a universal system of truth, one that takes in both nature and the supernatural, history and eternity. He does not have the material nor the tools with which to build such an all-encompassing synthesis. Neither can he hope to create a cosmic system of meaning, one that spans the spectrum of all the dimensions of meaning within man's experience or even all the motif contexts within the religious context of meaning. The theologian does not possess a superior point of view that allows him to transcend the presuppositional limits that are laid down in his material. His interest cannot be metaphysical; it must be historical. He cannot aim to develop a higher faith, only to understand the faith that is there before him. In the case of Christian theology, specifically, the theologian's interest must simply be to understand and explicate the characteristic nature of historical Christian faith.

Third, in the consideration of theological method, Nygren must again avoid all implications of metaphysics if he is to establish theology as a scientific discipline. In practice this means two things: that the method cannot be a speculative one, built on the assumptions of conceptual realism or functioning as a tool for ontological constructions; and that the method cannot simply be taken over from another discipline of science, whether within the area of religious studies or in another context of meaning altogether. These are not really restrictions, to Nygren's way of looking; they are rather fundamental guidelines as to the kind of method that scientific theology must develop. If the theological object of study is a given historical faith, and if the theologian's interest is to understand and explicate the characteristic motifs of this faith, then the method must clearly be a historical method, a historical-critical method, or a historical-systematic method. The dogmatic or systematic theologian does not engage in speculation, but in investigation. And his investigation is of a particular kind; it is not such that it falls under the sphere of any other science, within the area of religious studies or in any other context, or such that it can utilize the methods of any other discipline of study, religious or otherwise. The inquiry into the doctrinal characteristics of Christianity and the systematic structure of Christian faith requires a particular scientific method, namely motif research.

Parallel with Nygren's desire to avoid the methodological pitfalls of metaphysics stands his commitment to steer clear of subjectivism. Nygren's aversion to subjectivism also affects his views throughout—and in the context of theology the effects are evident in the consideration of the theological object of study, in the theologian's interest, and in the theological method.

We have observed earlier how Nygren understands the nature of subjectivism. What disqualifies it in the scientific context is the arbitrariness, the solipsism, the unverifiability and non-testability which typify the subjectivistic approach to things. Although subjectivism is often combined with metaphysics, its particular fallacy is in some ways the opposite of that of metaphysics. While metaphysics insists on overstepping the bounds of experience altogether, subjectivism locks itself behind the doors of individual experience. And while metaphysics is like a quick-footed fox jumping across the fences between different contexts of meaning and language, trying to catch what he can in any and all contexts, subjectivism is like a hedgehog that is curled up behind his own bristling coat, alone in his own little world of discourse. In the area of theology, as in science at large, subjectivism represents the denial of common sense and the privatization of reason, and all such tendencies are clearly illegitimate in the light of philosophical criticism. A discipline of study must be guided by the rules of science—or else left alone as one does the games of children, as innocent ignorance and not science.

Nygren's aversion to subjectivism forces him to define the theological object of study in positivistic ways. He cannot, in the first place, allow the theologian to focus on his own individual faith. Theology cannot be a scientific discipline if its object of study is not objectively given or if it is not available except to an individual. No science can exist if there is no intersubjectivity, no checks and balances, no possibility for sharing and testing knowledge. In the second place, Nygren cannot make the internal psychology or spirituality of belief, whether individual or corporate, the theological object of study. Such interiority is much too mystical, and much too unstable, to be analyzed and described by way of consistent scientific categories. Nygren has nothing against the phenomenological approach as such, but the phenomena to be studied must be available for study, not secret; they must be concrete, not ephemeral. There may be disciplines of study—as for example the psychology of religion —which can make the religious *subject* their subject matter, but theology is not such a discipline. Theology studies faith, not the believer; it focuses on historical-empirical manifestations of faith, not subjective-psychological dynamics of belief. The theological object of study lies in the *realizations* of religion—and in the case of Christian theology, specifically, in the historical realizations of Christian faith and thought, i.e., in the doctrinal traditions of Christianity.

For Nygren, the subjectivistic fallacy must be avoided in regard to the theologian's interest as well. The scientific theologian cannot be oriented to the propagation of his own faith or to changing the faith which he studies. His subjective convictions do of course play a role in motivating his endeavors and informing him with a sense of urgency and relevance. But his purposes are not those of a preacher or a prophet—not the proclamation of his own conceptions of the message or the formulation of a new word of God. If he is subjectively engaged, it is in the faith of the fathers. If he says things in a new way, they are the things that have always been there, implicit in the tradition which he studies. His responsibility as a theologian is to be a scholar of the faith, sensitive to the meaning of the faith, informed of the traditions of the faith, and skillful in the explication of the faith. His interest is always in the faith, in the essential nature of the faith and the characteristic motifs of the faith that lie lodged in the community of faith and in the traditions of faith—and in the case of the Christian theologian, particularly, in the Christian community and the Christian tradition.

Finally, the effect of subjectivism must be cleansed from the theological method also. Nygren cannot hope to give Christian dogmatics or systematic theology a scientific status if he cannot define its method in terms of scientific objectivity. No matter how successfully subjectivism has been avoided in the definition of the theological object of study or the theologian's interest, if it still influences the theological method the discipline is discredited among the sciences. Subjectivism in method shows itself in various ways. It may affect the selection of the material to be studied. The Christian theologian who is to investigate the Christian faith in order to identify and bring together its characteristic motifs cannot of course include everything that has ever been said and done as an expression of this faith. He must make a representative selection. But the selection must be just that—representative. He must not show any bias as to the particular sources or viewpoints which are to be included; any prejudice in the selection of evidence will result in a biased understanding and a slanted interpretation. Then, subjectivism may affect the formulation of hypotheses as well. A certain subjectivism in hypotheses may in fact be said to be inevitable.

The theologian must be guided by certain conceptual theories, otherwise he will have no way to identify any order, or pattern, or structure in the material he studies. But the hypotheses must be just that—hypotheses. They must always be tentative, always open to reassessment, always "softer" than the material to which they are applied. Any arbitrariness or absolutism in hypotheses will result in an arbitrary or absolutistic interpretation—and in the ultimate misrepresentation of the faith.

We have completed our summary of Nygren's views of the general qualities which theology, Christian theology, and especially Christian dogmatics or systematic theology must possess if it is to find a place in the society of science which forms its cultural context at the present. But this chapter covers only part of the picture. We have considered only the general requirements or principal restrictions which, in Nygren's view, a scientific theology must fulfill. We shall proceed next to observe how, positively, he goes about fulfilling the requirements and constructing the discipline for which he desires to claim full and equal status among the sciences—systematic theology.

VII. The Science of Faith

Before we examine some principal aspects of Nygren's definition of the subject matter of scientific theology, it may be helpful to recapitulate a few central points in the analysis of his philosophy of religion. These will not only be important in trying to understand the internal connections of Nygren's thought, and in this context particularly the continuity between his philosophical perspectives and his theological methodology; they will help us also avoid unnecessary repetition and duplication of points as we go along.

As we have seen, the relationship between philosophy and theology according to Nygren is that between a science of universals and a science of particulars. Philosophy is that science of principles whose primary function is the logical analysis of fundamental presuppositions of meaning and validity. It seeks to identify these presuppositions in terms of a series of formal transcendental categories which underlie the various contexts of meaning that are evident in human experience and in the institutions of human society. Religion is one of these contexts of meaning, as is manifest both in the fact that the fundamental question of eternity engages men universally and in the fact that the religious consciousness produces a variety of institutional expressions in culture and society. Philosophy of religion is that branch of the science of universals which undertakes to analyze the phenomena that belong to the religious context of meaning for the purpose of identifying the formal presuppositional category or categories which govern this particular dimension of human experience. It is defined by Nygren as "the logical analysis of the fundamental presuppositions of religious meaning."

But religious meaning, although it belongs formally within a single categorical context, is not all expressed in the same way or in terms of a similar material content. The fundamental religious question is clearly distinguishable from other presuppositional questions, but it does not call forth an unequivocal or uniform answer. In actuality, religion appears in many forms, with a variety of content, and with different meaning among different people. There is, in fact, no universal religion, only particular religions, each characterized by a different conception of what the religious question means and what the answer ultimately must be.

In his study of religious phenomena, the philosopher of religion is not concerned with particular answers but with the nature of the religious question. He seeks to penetrate the particular to get at the universal. On the other hand, when he undertakes to identify the presuppositional category, the philosopher does not define it as a universal norm by which particular religions are to be judged or evaluated. Instead, he defines the universal religious category in such a way as to leave the particular religions intact, included within the open presuppositional form which the universal category is. The philosopher's primary interest is to analyze the presuppositions which underlie human religion as such, not to describe the particular motifs or motif structures which are characteristic of each individual religion.

The study of particular religions—of the many motif contexts that are in evidence in the religious context of meaning—is the responsibility of a science of particulars, namely theology. While the study of universals is a philosophical science, operating by way of logical analysis, the study of particulars is a historical science, operating by way of historical-critical analysis. While philosophy of religion aims to identify the structure of the general presuppositional context of religious meaning, theology aims to identify the structure of particular motif contexts which exist wherever the religious question is being asked and answered in actuality. Christianity is one of many such particular motif contexts which exist among men. Christian theology is that discipline which studies the particular motif structure that characterizes Christianity—the one among the many historical religions which is most meaningful to the Christian theologian or which is most relevant to the cultural situation within which he stands.

Theology, then, as Nygren defines it, has a specific task that is related to a particular faith; it is, in short, the science of faith. But this must be understood correctly. Faith is only the subject matter of theology, not the starting point for theological insight. Theology is not a speculative or theoretical discipline, but a historical and analytical one. It does not aim toward a higher metaphysical knowledge or start with special religious insight; it aims toward historical-critical understanding and starts with a scientific frame of mind. Faith is what the scientific theologian studies, not his mind set; his mind set is science, and the faith he studies is a historical-empirical phenomenon, a positive entity, an object available for objective research.

This is as far as we have brought our analysis of Nygren's theological methodology so far. We must now consider more closely his definition of the theological object of study.

THE SUBJECTIVITY AND OBJECTIVITY OF FAITH

It is obvious that Nygren's concern for the scientific reputation of theology has been determinative for his definition of the theological object of study. If the fallacies of metaphysics and subjectivism are to be avoided, they must be avoided in the conception of the subject matter of theology as well as in the delineation of the theologian's interest and in his decisions concerning theological method. Nygren has thus been forced to open up a chasm between faith as a subjective standpoint, or as the basis for a reflective superstructure of theology, on the one hand, and faith as a historical phenomenon, or as the object of scientific investigation, on the other. For Nygren, clearly, subjective faith-reflection does not qualify as a scientific discipline; only the historical-critical investigation of the objective expressions of faith does.

But is the problem of subjectivism thereby solved? Even if Nygren succeeds in freeing the theologian from the subjective faith perspective, is not this perspective still present in the material which he studies—in religious experience, in the historical-empirical phenomena, in the faith-reflection which is expressed in religious traditions and institutions? Is not all religion fundamentally conditioned by subjectivity and therefore by definition unscientific?

Nygren struggles with this problem—he calls it "the sore spot" of his methodology.[1] He can separate scientific theology from faith-reflection, and he can remove subjectivism from the mind set of the scientific theologian, but he cannot deny the subjectivity of the material which the scientific theologian studies. What possibility is there for an objective scientific study of subjectively conditioned material?

Nygren's answer takes the form of an elemental logical analysis of the concepts of subjectivity and objectivity.[2] He makes an attempt to sort out the various types of subjectivity/objectivity polarity which are commonly associated with these concepts, and seeks to determine whether the subjectivity which is involved in religious experience would necessarily compromise the objectivity of the investigation of the material manifestations of religious faith. His analysis runs as follows: [3]

Subjectivity and objectivity are not unequivocal concepts. Set over against each other they may, in fact, refer to a whole series of logical polarities: empirical-existential awareness versus thing-in-itself; psychical impressions versus physical objects; value-conscious versus value-free; and arbitrary versus necessary. When one charges theology with subjectivity, or aims to establish its objectivity, one should make clear which of these logical polarities one has in mind. Not all of them are equally applicable at every point—in fact, if theology were to be defined in terms of an objectivity that relates to the polarity of thing-in-itself over against empirical-existential awareness, the effect might well be that the scientific qualities of theology were compromised because of objectivity! It is rather dangerous, therefore, to leave the concepts of subjectivity and objectivity undefined; the argument can then easily slip from one set of polarities to another under the cloak of the general ambiguity of the two concepts, and the net effect is logical equivocation and total confusion of the issue.

Which of the logical polarities within the subjectivity/objectivity dialectic are at work in the case of the theological object of study, then? What precisely is the type of subjectivity which would disqualify the theological investigation of faith from obtaining rank among the objective sciences? In Nygren's view, the first three of the polarities mentioned are not at all relevant to the case. If the faith which is to be studied is defined in terms of historical-empirical phenomena, it makes no sense at all to question whether this material represents empirical-existential awareness or the-thing-itself. The material is there, concretely given and available for research, regardless. And the same is the case whether the material is judged to be value-conscious or value-free. Both of these kinds of material must be taken into view if the theologian is to be regarded as a responsible scientist in his field. The fact that there is existential subjectivity, psychical impressions, or value consciousness involved in the experience of faith does not in any way disqualify the historical-empirical manifestations of faith as an object of scientific study. On the contrary, if all such materials were to be left out of consideration altogether, the study of religious faith could hardly be called scientific.

Thus, in regard to the theological object of study, the only aspect of the subjectivity/objectivity dialectic which has a bearing on the scientific status of the discipline is the logical polarity between arbitrary and necessary. The question comes down to this: Is the theologian relating to all the material necessary to his inquiry, or is he in any way biased by subjective or arbitrary interests in the selection of material? Does the material which is selected belong within the purview of theology as by an unbroken continuum of logical necessity, or is it in any way haphazardly chosen or arbitrarily limited? In answering this question, Nygren develops the following explanation of the logical continuum within which Christian theology stands:[4]

1. Philosophy of religion analyzes the historical content of human religion for the purpose of identifying the formal presuppositional category that underlies all religious meaning and validity, of whatever form.
2. Christian theology investigates the historical content of Christian faith for the purpose of identifying the characteristic motifs that inform the Christian understanding of religious meaning particularly.
3. Specific disciplines of Christian theology examine various manifestations of Christian faith and life for the purpose of identifying the essential nature of Christianity.

As one can see, the continuum appears as a tight logical structure. The only point where a break could possibly occur is at step 2, where the Christian theologian seems arbitrarily to limit himself to the historical content of Christian faith. To Nygren's mind, however, this cannot be sufficient cause for charging Christian theology with arbitrariness. It is a matter of necessity for *Christian* theology, if it is to be both scientific and Christian, to investigate Christian faith. When one recalls, in addition, that Nygren places Christianity on a par with other forms of religion, in a relative position as one among the many religions of man, then the preoccupation of the Christian theologian with the Christian faith is clearly set in relation to the preoccupation of other theologians with other faiths, and in no case is there any ground or intention to make dogmatic claims to absoluteness or normativity. The scientific study of Christian faith does not invalidate any other faith or preempt any other theology. Christian theology simply assumes its own task—its necessary task—as that particular scientific discipline which is responsible for the investigation and explication of the characteristic content and essential meaning of the Christian faith.

Nygren has thus successfully defended his discipline against the charge of methodological subjectivism. He has shown that scientific theology can legitimately be Christian theology. But he has not thereby solved the practical problem of subjectivity —the difficulty with which the scientific theologian is faced as a result of the profusion of theologies, individual and corporate, sectarian and ecclesiastical, which are part of the historical-empirical material of Christian theology. Nygren has yet to explain how the scientific investigation of historical Christian faith can also legitimately be called "systematic theology." This is the question which must be considered next.

THE HISTORICAL CONSISTENCY OF FAITH

When the Christian theologian confronts the historical-empirical material which constitutes his object of study, he is immediately aware of its great complexity, and especially of the many different varieties of viewpoints, interpretations, and doctrinal emphases which have been worked into Christian faith traditions by various people and at various times along the way. It is his task to identify and explicate the characteristic content and essential meaning of Christian faith, but before him lies a material that seems more characteristic of a Paul, a John, an Origen, a Tertullian, an Augustine, an Aquinas, or a Luther than of any single, unified Christian "type," or that seems more expressive of the standpoints of a number of different traditions and schools, Catholic and Protestant, than of the point of view of the Christian tradition as a whole. The question, simply stated, is whether there is any integrity or consistency to historical Christian faith at all.

Nygren has two principal ways of answering this question. The first is in terms of what he calls "the role of the self-evident in history"; the other is in terms of what he calls "the contrast between atomism and connection in the conception of history." [5] Both are designed to undergird the conviction that each individual religion, in spite of all superficial evidence to the contrary, represents a single motif context, a structure of meaning that has integrity and consistency and that can be identified and explicated by way of motif research.

Nygren argues that motif contexts are held together and governed by certain basic, unifying presuppositions, precisely the way the major presuppositional contexts—the category contexts—are, though with certain differences in the way the presuppositions function. In the primary contexts of meaning the presuppositions are necessary; they have the force of *logical necessity*. In the secondary contexts of meaning—the motif contexts—the presuppositions are self-evident; they have only what we might call *hermeneutical inevitability*. In one sense, of course, the concepts "necessary" and "self-evident" are synonymous—"logically necessary presuppositions" are also "self-evident," and "self-evident hermeneutical presuppositions" are also "necessary." But there is a fine distinction between them which Nygren is anxious to observe. The logically necessary presuppositions that govern the religious context of meaning as a whole can be shown to be necessary by way of logical analysis. The hermeneutically inevitable presuppositions which govern a particular motif context, on the other hand, are not logically demonstrable as being inevitable. It is not possible to prove that a certain motif context or motif structure is the only possible hermeneutical presupposition in the field of religious meaning. Another person or group of persons may start with an altogether different motif presupposition, one that seems self-evident and inevitable to them, and there is no way to refute them.

In spite of the distinction between necessary and self-evident presuppositions, however, Nygren is convinced that they are both at work, at different levels, within each particular type of religion or faith. They inform the historical-empirical material which the theologian studies—the first, formally, as the framework of religious meaning in general; the second, materially, as the structure of each religious type, individually—and they are both analyzable on the basis of the material.

As an illustration of what is involved in confronting a certain religious motif context such as Christianity, Nygren submits an analysis of a correlative case, namely the historian's approach to the interpretation of a historical period of the past. The historian's aim is, of course, to describe things "exactly as they were." But that is not at all simple. Not only are the sources at times contradictory, so as to require sifting and sorting. There are deeper difficulties involved, some that are tied in with the self-evident presuppositions which are at work in the material, and some that are related to the self-evident presuppositions which are at work in the historian himself. As Nygren says, "Every age has that which it accepts as self-evident, and it is this that sets the profoundest mark on an age." [6]

In confronting the task of interpreting a certain historical period, the most common procedure among historians is to focus on the ideas and concepts which are most clearly in contention with each other during the era in question. The intellectual conflicts which occur are considered formative for the age, being the roots from which groups and parties, sects and movements grow. Historians, therefore, tend to focus on the most controversial issues of the period they study. But in so doing they easily overlook the deeper things that determine the real character of the age—the self-evident presuppositions on which the entire culture is built and which are held in common by all parties to every conflict, friend and foe alike. These seldom become the subject of discussion; they are the basis for the discussion. They are seldom examined; they are taken for granted, assumed as valid. They are, as Nygren says, "like the air we breathe, the atmosphere in which we live." [7]

But it is here that the historian is faced with his most difficult dilemma. He himself is part of one era and the material he studies belongs to another. He cannot avoid the self-evident presuppositions of his own age; but the material cannot be understood except on the basis of the self-evident presuppositions which dominate its age. How shall the historian proceed? By merging his own viewpoint with that of the material and make its self-evident presuppositions his own? That may seem the ideal procedure, but the situation is not really solved by a procedure that simple. For in immersing himself so completely in a past era that its assumptions and ideas become his own, the historian loses the perspective—that distance from the material—without which historical understanding is itself impossible. The dilemma, in Nygren words, is this: "The very thing that constitutes the historian's chief difficulty is the very thing that is prerequisite to the historical perspective."[8] Obviously, the historian needs both closeness to and distance from his material. If closeness is lacking, he has no perception on which to build an understanding—the historian then easily becomes the victim of what Nygren calls "anachronism." But if he is too close, so that the assumptions of his material are his own assumptions as well, then he ceases to be a historian altogether.

How then can one make sure that the self-evident presuppositions of a particular period of history or a certain motif context of religion are understood correctly? If these presuppositions are in fact operative on the level of unquestioned assumptions, and are not usually made explicit or obvious, how can the historian learn to respect them, or even to observe them, and guard against arbitrarily imposing his own set of assumptions or presuppositions on the material? Nygren's answer is this: The material itself will resist the imposition of perspectives that are foreign to its own presuppositions. There is an integrity or a consistency that belongs to the historical-empirical material itself—what Nygren calls "the stubbornness of the facts."[9] If the historian approaches his subject matter on the basis of assumptions or perspectives that are alien to the material, he will soon discover that the facts are against him. He will be forced to submit the facts to all sorts of violence in order to make them fit his perspectives. If, on the other hand, he has grasped the presuppositions of the material itself, his conception is corroborated by the facts, and there is no need to force the evidence to fit the perspective. It will all seem right.

At this point Nygren unveils his conviction that the assumption of an inner connection and consistency in a certain system of thought is a safer and more useful one than the opposite assumption of atomistic disconnection and internal contradiction. Historical-critical research is often undertaken solely for the purpose of dissecting the constituent parts of a thought system and analyzing each element separately—and usually in terms of their "biological particularity" or the "genealogical connections" that can be established between individual thoughts and other thought systems which may have had an influence on the system in question. A system of thought is thus often analyzed into dissolution—appearing as a mass of dissimilar ideas that cancel each other out or at least are shown to be incapable of combination. Nygren questions such procedures. Is it really credible that a great thinker or a major thought system of the past was less aware of the fundamental requirements of logic than the historical analyst in the present? Is it not more reasonable—or at least methodologically more profitable—to assume that the contradictions and inconsistencies which we discover are a sign that we have not understood the material on the basis of the presuppositions which underlie it, but have instead forced an alien set of assumptions on it? The questions are, of course, quite rhetorical. In Nygren's view, the appearance of contradictions in a given system of thought ought to bring the interpreter to dig deeper and check his assumptions. One must simply assume that "an interpretation which makes unified sense of an outlook is more likely to be right than one which can do no more than represent it as an array of contradictions." [10] Not until the systematic structure of a system of thought is grasped is the system in fact understood.

But how, specifically, is the systematic structure of a religious motif context, a historical type of faith, determined? Does the historical Christian faith, for example, itself contain the means of its systematic integration? It is in order to answer these questions that we must now, finally, turn to Nygren's view of the role of the *grundmotiv*—the basic motif—in structuring an integrated system of faith.

THE INTEGRITY OF FAITH

As we have already seen, it is Nygren's conviction that each individual religion represents a religious type, a separate motif context, a unique motif structure that is integrated and consistent within itself and that can be understood as a totality and interpreted as a unity. This conviction is ultimately grounded in the analysis of the two presuppositional contexts within which any and all religious material must be interpreted, namely the primary category context and the secondary motif context.[11] It is all part of the twofold relationship—the logical and the hermeneutical—which exists between categorical questions and historical answers.

At this point an important emphasis in Nygren's methodology must be recalled. Nygren is namely concerned that we understand the exact *structure* of the logical relationship between the general religious context of meaning and the presuppositional categories which underlie it, and that we observe the precise *dynamics* of the hermeneutical interaction betwen general religious questions and particular religious answers. In principle, one could say that the systematic integrity of a particular faith is guaranteed in two ways: first by the fact that it is an answer to a *question,* and secondly by the fact that it is an *answer* to a question. In the first instance the organizing principle or integrating factor is the categorical presupposition—the formal religious question. In the second instance the systematic factor or unifying force is the motif presupposition—the material religious answer. Since both of these presuppositions are at work within any given religious type, one can legitimately say that the systematic integrity of a certain type of faith is grounded *both* in the fundamental presupposition of all religious meaning, *and* in the particular presupposition which governs this particular interpretation of religious meaning.

But here it is important to observe precisely how the relationship between the categorical question and the material answer is structured. Nygren has said that they belong together and affect each other, logically and hermeneutically. He has emphasized also that they must be kept distinct and not be mixed together or confused. The principal formula is this: Questions and answers must be held together without being confused; they must be distinguished from one another without being separated. We can now understand why. If, for instance, the question and answer were identical, each particular historical faith would be both an answer and a question—which is solipsism, confusion, disintegration. If, on the other hand, the question and the answer were torn apart, each individual historical faith would be an answer without a question—which is atomism, nonsense, and again disintegration. In either case the basic guarantees of the systematic integrity of a particular faith would be voided. It is only by distinguishing between question and answer, and at the same time relating them to one another as question and answer, that the systematic integrity of a particular system of faith can be secured. The bottom line, simply stated, is this: an answer has integrity, first by being related to a *question*, then by being in fact an *answer*.

When Nygren finally comes to consider what it is that ultimately determines the systematic structure of the faith content of a particular religion, he is led to give priority to the internal, intentional core of the motif structure. He says:

> Even when we know that as regards its form a historical faith is an answer to a question that belongs to the religious category, we can give no clear account of its content, nor indeed any account at all, unless we know also the fundamental motif which gives it its distinctive character and determines its meaning.[12]

Nygren defines this fundamental motif, the *grundmotiv* of a particular religious faith, as "the fundamental answer which it gives to a question of a categorical nature, and by which its individual judgments, valuations and decisions are held together in a meaningful unity."[13] Here indeed is the ultimate principle of systematic integration within a historical faith. It is by reference to the *grundmotiv*, the basic idea, the central concept, or the fundamental thought, that the many and varied expressions of faith—propositional or otherwise—that belong to a particular historical religion derive their distinctive character and are held together in a unique system of religious meaning. The fundamental motif is that factor which constitutes the context—the motif context—as a material unity and gives consistency, structure, and systematic integrity to a particular historical type of faith. It is therefore, clearly, the crucial element in the theologian's object of study—the Rosetta stone which he must first and above all else make it his ambition to find.

But when the fundamental motif of a certain faith is identified, the scientific theologian is still only part of the way toward the fulfillment of his systematic task. He must go on to identify the many subsidiary motifs which cluster around the central motif and through which the *grundmotif* is developed and expressed, and he must finally attempt to show how these thoughts or affirmations are related to one another and to the central motif. Motif research is thus itself a systematic endeavor. The scientific theologian is not called upon to create a system, but to analyze the system which is given within the material itself. As Nygren says, the Christian theologian is not there to "produce any external systematization, but rather to allow the Christian faith to be seen in its own inner organic coherence." [14] Motif research is thus "the most important part of systematic theology."

> It is fundamental in the sense that it lays the foundation on which everything else rests. If motif research succeeds in clarifying the fundamental Christian motif, then the problems of systematic theology are in principle solved. For the answer is thereby given to the question of the essential character of the Christian faith, which is the chief and all-controlling question of systematic theology. What systematic theology has to do beyond this is simply to draw out in different directions the implications already present in the fundamental Christian motif.[15]

And with that the scene is set for our consideration of the method of motif research itself.

VIII. Motif Research

Whenever Anders Nygren's theological method is referred to, it is called, for short, "the method of motif research." It is a good description. Everything Nygren has ever done in regard to theological methodology comes to focus in the concept of motif research. But the phrase itself covers a wide area. In a general sense it can stand for the entire complex of philosophical, theoretical and methodological ideas which Nygren has developed as background for his definition of scientific systematic theology; in a narrower sense it refers to the actual procedure by which the systematic theologian undertakes the historical-critical investigation of the characteristic motifs of Christian faith. In the first sense motif research encompasses everything that is contained in the five preceding chapters of this book; in the second sense it has to do with the process that results in an understanding of essential Christianity such as the one which is presented in the next section.

When we come to focus on the method of motif research in this chapter, it is with the second, more practical or procedural aspect of Nygren's methodology that we are concerned. As we have seen, one of the requirements of a scientific discipline of study is that it has a method that is appropriate to its material

—its object of study—and to its interests—the objectives of its study. The method, moreover, must be characterized by objectivity, intersubjectivity, and testability. Nygren is concerned to establish systematic theology—the discipline which studies a certain historical-empirical type of faith in the interest of identifying its unique character and essential meaning—with status as a scientific discipline. He must therefore show that the systematic theologian has available an objective method of research that is appropriate to the investigation of historical religion and that is capable of getting at the core and essence of the faith it studies. As Nygren looks at it, the method must be a historical method; it must be a historical-critical method; and it must be a historical-systematic method. It is precisely in reference to these three qualities that he develops his method of motif research.

A HISTORICAL METHOD

That the scientific systematic theologian must have a historical method is clear from the nature of the material which he studies. His material is historical; his method must be historical, also. Nygren argues, in fact, not only that motif research is *a* historical method, but that it is *the historical method par excellence*. Motif research is simply more truly historical than any other approach to historical research.

To support this rather extraordinary contention, Nygren undertakes to examine what he calls "the way to historical understanding."[1] By way of a simple illustration, (cf. diagram), he explains the principal difference between the two most common approaches to historical understanding—that which he describes as the "chronicle" approach and that which he describes as the "caricature" approach. And he shows that when they both go the full cycle of historical investigation, each in its separate course, they eventually come together and reach their highest potential in terms of motif research. The process is described as follows:

Nygren first notes that history starts, not with facts but with the interpretation of facts. Before history there is only the multitude of unrelated events, objects, and individuals that mingle in the chaos of factual reality. In Nygren's view there is no such thing as "history as actuality"; the phrase is a misnomer. The chaos of atomistic facts is not, as such, history. History occurs only as there is a selection, an ordering, a structuring, and an interpretation, or as the facts are dealt with by way of a historical perspective that is superimposed on the chaotic raw material by the historian. And once there is history there is no longer mere actuality.

The historian, in his attempt to gain mastery over the factual chaos, has two options—two opposite ways to approach his task. On the one hand, he can attempt to recount as fully as possible all the individual elements that belong within the manifold of human experience. This is the chronicle approach—what historians at times call "history as record." On the other hand, he can proceed to place in focus certain striking features in the manifold elements that are particularly interesting or unique. This is the caricature approach—what historians at times refer to as "history as writing." As different as these two approaches are, Nygren does not consider them different in principle. Both are ways of facing the problem of history, and

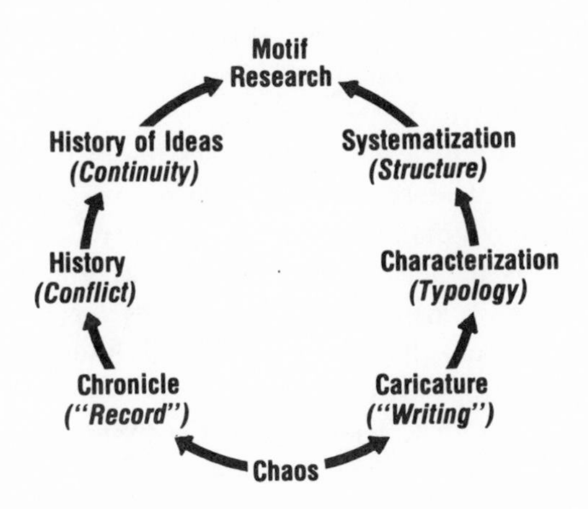

both attempt to solve it by way of certain processes of selection. The difference is relative, related to the criteria by which the selection process is guided.

The *chronicle,* on the one hand, cannot possibly hope to be all inclusive. It can never be fully representative of all the given facts. The chronicler cannot possibly recount everything that ever happened. Even if he should seek to list everything, the list is simply *his* listing, not everything that could have been listed. The *caricature,* on the other hand, is an acknowledgment of the impossibility of completeness and a decision to try an alternate approach. Even if the historian cannot record everything, he can note that which is most striking or most unusual in the chaos of experience—or at least that which seems most interesting to his own mind. The difference between the chronicle and the caricature is not that the one gives an exact picture of reality while the other is a distortion. This, says Nygren, is simply a misconception of the nature of historical understanding. Both approaches seek to give expression to that which is given in experience and reality, and both present the material in their own way—reworked and transformed according to the historian's best judgment. The difference is simply that the chronicle gives primary attention to that which is average and normal, while the caricature gives primary attention to that which is unique and unusual. The one approach is not on principle any more to be preferred than the other.

There is one basic weakness which affects both of these approaches to historical understanding, namely, the subjectivity and arbitrariness which so easily beset their treatment of the factual material. The error of the chronicler is not that he makes a selection among the things to be recorded—this he must do if he is to accomplish anything at all. The error is that the selection is arbitrary. The error of the caricature, on the other hand, is not that it focuses on the unusual—this may be necessary if one desires to grasp the contours of that reality which is to be presented. The error is, once more, that the focus is arbitrary. In order to overcome the problem of subjectivism and arbitrariness it is necessary that the historian develop viewpoints that are more objective and more essential. And this happens, in both lines of approach, when the perspectives are raised from the level of chronicle and caricature to the level of history and characterization.

History or historical reflection, as Nygren defines it, is that perspective which attempts to place the factual material not simply on a chronicler's record but under viewpoints that are central to the material itself—in historical context. *Characterization* or typological interpretation, on the other hand, is an endeavor to grasp not simply what seems unusual or striking from the standpoint of caricature but what is characteristic of a person, an entity, or an event—what is the essential uniqueness of the material itself. In both approaches to historical understanding, the attempt is made to overcome the effects of subjective arbitrariness by placing the facts within a larger context or by going beyond the level of atomistic observations to more objective and inclusive perspectives. This is an important point to observe. Nygren refers to a common misconception which is abroad among historians that the chronicle, with its intention to reproduce reality faithfully, stands closer to the truth than history, which applies a more inclusive viewpoint and therefore moves further away from reality itself. To Nygren's way of thinking, the exact opposite is the case. "Each step further in the historical direction means a closer approximation to the immediately given reality. It is an attempt to neutralize the error that was committed in the first reworking and transformation [of the factual material]."[2] Thus, what appears superficially to be a withdrawal from the immediately given reality is in point of fact the way to come closer to the truth about it.

At this point, however, yet another level of historical interpretation comes into view—and on both sides of the methodological scheme. There is clearly a need for an even larger and more inclusive perspective if the subjectivism and arbitrariness of the lower levels are to be overcome entirely. On the level of history or historical context, on the one hand, historical understanding is limited to the immediate chronological setting—in the case of events, contemporaneity, and in the case of persons, biography. In order to break out of this imprisonment of time it is necessary that events, persons or ideas are placed within a larger—or perhaps longer—context, namely within the kind of continuity through time which marks historical evolution or the history of ideas. And something similar must take place, in the other line of approach, with characterization or typological interpretation. The attempt to identify what is central or essential in an event, an entity, or a person, cannot ultimately succeed as long as each individual unit is considered in isolation. Individual types must be placed within a larger and more inclusive context; characterization must give way to systematization.

The *history of ideas,* as Nygren describes it, is that perspective which places individual facts and separate historical contexts in continuity with one another. While history places the facts that are contained in the chronicle within what might be called a latitudinal setting, history of ideas provides in addition a longitudinal orientation. *Systematization,* on the other side, does generally the same thing with caricature and characterization. It is only when individual characteristics or typological differences are seen in a larger systematic context that the essential uniqueness of each unit or each type can be identified and understood. Once more we observe how Nygren's methodological principle works: the victory over subjectivity and arbitrariness—and the actual approximation to truth—is not accomplished by reverting to observations of individual, atomistic facts, whether as chronicle or caricature, but by moving to larger and more inclusive connections or contexts. And the final step in this quest for objectivity, both for the chronicle-history-history of ideas approach and for the caricature-characterization-systematization approach, is the elevation of the historian's perspective to the level of motif research.

Motif research, as Nygren describes it here, is that perspective on history which places the historical material, derived by either of the two approaches to historical interpretation, within the most inclusive context possible. Motif research takes the material that belongs to chronicle, history, and the history of ideas all the way to the level of ultimate, universal presuppositions—to the fundamental contexts of meaning which govern all awareness and all understanding, of whatever sort. Likewise, motif research takes the material that is derived from caricature, characterization, and systematization to the absolute highest level of systematization—to the fundamental categories of meaning in which the structure of human experience and human behavior is ultimately determined. On this level of historical understanding, all subjectivity and arbitrariness are dissolved. Yet, while applying the most objective and inclusive perspectives possible, motif research has not removed itself from the factual phenomena or from the realities of actual existence. On the contrary. Says Nygren, "The viewpoint which motif research adopts is more objectively inescapable and anchored in 'the historical material' itself than any of the other viewpoints which might be adopted in the study of history." [3] Once more, Nygren emphasizes that it is the more inclusive perspective that comes the closest to the truth. Motif research, in applying the most inclusive perspective possible—the perspective of categorical presuppositions—is therefore the crowning point of the historical method. In it meet and are brought to completion all the avenues of historical understanding. Motif research is the historical method *par excellence.*

A HISTORICAL-CRITICAL METHOD

But Nygren is not satisfied with the characterization of motif research as a historical method. This level of historical understanding, the highest, where one is operating within the perspectives of categorical presuppositions, is clearly both philosophically and historically oriented. The method which the scientific systematic theologian uses must, therefore, be characterized as a historical-critical method.

Nygren has indicated on several occasions that motif research could just as well be described as "typological research" or "structural research." [4] His intentions in these contexts have clearly been to identify motif research with those approaches to historical study which are concerned with larger contexts and connections, and to distinguish it from the kind of historic-genetic research which is interested merely in observing facts and tracing their causal relations with one another. The latter is the approach that Nygren finds dominant in modern theology and in the scientific study of religion, generally, and he considers it altogether inadequate. History of religion and history of doctrine are clear examples of this, to Nygren's way of thinking. These disciplines have become preoccupied with tracing derivations of doctrine and drawing parallels between religious ideas. Not that these endeavors are unimportant; such studies make indispensable contributions to the science of faith. But in comparison to structural research, or motif research, they are nonetheless secondary. The orientation is simply too peripheral. One does not understand a certain doctrine by observing its different elements or tracing their genetic derivations. Neither does one understand a certain historical religion by analyzing its individual ideas or comparing them with similar ideas in other faiths. In a statement that amounts to a final squaring of accounts with historic-genetic research, Nygren says:

> The most important task of those engaged in the modern scientific study of religion and in theological research is to reach an inner understanding of the different forms of religion in the light of their different fundamental motifs. For a long time they have been chiefly occupied in collecting a vast mass of material drawn from different religious sources for the purpose of comparison. But when the comparison actually comes to be made, the uncertainty of it immediately becomes apparent; for it is plain that no conclusion can be drawn from the mere fact that one and the same idea or belief occurs in different religious contexts. The idea or belief may have exactly the same form without having at all the same meaning, if in one case it is a basic conception, while in the other it is more loosely attached. Its meaning cannot be the same if—as is naturally most often the case—its setting is different in the different religions. What such an idea, or belief, or sentiment really means can only be decided in the light of its

> own natural context. In other words, we must try to see what is the basic idea or the driving power in the religion concerned, or what it is that gives it its character as a whole and communicates to all its parts their special content and color. It is the attempt to carry out such structural analysis, whether in the sphere of religion or elsewhere, that we describe as motif research.[5]

Nygren's reference to the natural context of the idea, belief, or sentiment that is studied is important in our context here. It refers to the twofold presuppositional framework within which all historical-empirical material belongs and which we have seen Nygren describe as the primary or category context, on the one hand, and the secondary or motif context, on the other.[6] It has to do, first, with the *logical* connection between the religious context of meaning and the general presuppositional category of religion, and second, with the *hermeneutical* connection between the general religious category—the formal question—and the particular historical type of religion—the material answer. As Nygren defines motif research, it is that method of historical inquiry which approaches its material from the perspectives of its relationship, first, to the general religious category of meaning, and second, to the particular motif structure which characterizes the faith in question.

But when this is said, it must obviously be questioned whether Nygren, in fact, accepts the notion of the complete equivalence between typological research and structural research, on the one hand, and motif research, on the other. In our examination of Nygren's analysis of the way to historical understanding, we have seen him refer to typology as equivalent with characterization—the second-level perspective in the caricature approach to historical understanding. We have seen his reference, also, to the larger systematic context—and thus by implication to systematic structure—on the systematization level of the same line of approach. It appears, therefore, that Nygren locates typological and structural research somewhere in the middle of the spectrum of historical understanding. If so, the relationship between typological research, structural research, and motif research appears to be the following: Typological research and structural research are methods of historical understanding that are conditioned purely by historical considerations; motif research, on the other hand, is a historical-critical method that is conditioned both by philosophical and historical considerations. Typological research and structural research are concerned with secondary *motif contexts* only; motif research sets the consideration of secondary motif contexts within the larger framework of the primary *category context.*

It appears, then, that Nygren is not really served by accepting typological research and structural research as altogether equivalent with motif research. True, they are the equivalents of *one aspect* of motif research—that which has to do with the character and structure of the particular motif context that is studied. But this, after all, is the less important of the two kinds of contexts which motif research is concerned with. To accept the equivalence of typological research, structural research, and motif research could therefore have some rather unfortunate consequences for Nygren. Not only could motif research be robbed of its unique position as a historical-critical method; scientific systematic theology could itself be reduced to a purely historical discipline, and it would then be difficult to defend its independent status and resist its absorption into such disciplines as the history of ideas or general historical-structural analysis. The scientific status of systematic theology would clearly be in jeopardy, because the uniqueness of its method would have been lost.

It is precisely in order to avoid this shrinking of theology into history, and motif reseach into structural research, that Nygren insists on the double conditioning of scientific theology and of motif research, its method. Theology does not study faith simply as a historical phenomenon, but as the *historical realization of the universal category of religion.* Motif research does not focus simply on the internal structure of religious events or thoughts, but on events and thoughts *as they are structured to answer categorical questions.* The reason motif research can be said to be the historical method *par excellence* is that it is not simply a historical method; it deals with its material, not only within the context of historical connections—the motif context—but also in the context of universal presuppositions—the category context. The latter is in fact its primary perspective. Motif research is uniquely a historical-critical method.

But not even that is sufficient to describe fully the method of motif research. It must be defined as a *historical-systematic* method as well. Nygren in fact argues that it is the historical-systematic method *par preference.*

A HISTORICAL-SYSTEMATIC METHOD

When Nygren talks about the natural context within which religious ideas, beliefs or sentiments are to be studied, he quickly goes on to emphasize that the theologian "must try to see what is the basic idea or the driving power in the religion concerned, or what it is that gives it its character as a whole and communicates to all its parts their special content and color." [7] Motif research cannot, in other words, be satisfied with identifying and summarizing all the separate ideas that belong within the motif context of a certain faith; it must go after "the fundamental motif," "the central idea," "the organizing principle," "the characteristic concept," "the essential meaning"—in short, the theologian must seek to identify the unifying force or the synthesizing factor within the faith he studies.[8]

As we have seen, Nygren defines the fundamental motif of a certain religion as "the fundamental answer which it gives to a question of a categorical nature and by which its individual judgments, valuations and decisions are held together in a meaningful unity." [9] The key concept here is "a question of a categorical nature." In seeking to identify the fundamental motif of a particular faith, motif research applies the most inclusive of all perspectives—the universal religious question. It is only in being considered an answer to such a categorical question that a historical faith reveals its essential characteristics.

We are here, once more, at the point where the double conditioning of motif research appears as the key to its methodological uniqueness. It is a historical method, but it is also a philosophical one; the question it asks is a philosophical question, and the answer it seeks is a historical answer. For Nygren, this double orientation of motif research is the guarantee of the scientific qualities of the method: the first guarantees its objectivity, the second assures its essentiality. Motif research is therefore not only the historical method *par excellence;* it must be considered the systematic method *par preference* as well.

But this is also where Nygren's method has been most seriously questioned—namely, in regard to its objectivity and its essentiality. Nygren is aware of this, and he has at various times and in different contexts addressed himself to a series of objections and questions raised by colleagues and critics.[10]

Interestingly, both scientific positivists and conservative dogmatists have raised objections to what they describe as "the overpowering and distorting of the material studied by way of an arbitrary imposition of categorical questions formulated by philosophy." The positivist claims that the material must be approached "without prejudice," in a "presuppositionless" manner; the dogmatist requires that the faith be approached "on its own presuppositions," not on the basis of philosophical questions. Nygren's answer can be summarized as follows: (1) Categorical questions are not arbitrary; they are rather in the nature of the case. (2) Categorical questions are not content-defined or slanted; on the contrary, they are formal questions, open to all the possibilities and variations in the historical material. (3) The positivist's "presuppositionlessness" is a myth; all historical interpretation requires a viewpoint. (4) The dogmatist's requirement that the material be interpreted by reference to "its own presuppositions" is only fulfilled when both categorical presuppositions and motif presuppositions are considered; this is exactly what motif research does. (5) The viewpoint which motif research adopts is both more objective and more closely related to the nature of the historical material than any other viewpoint that might be adopted.

But this last claim by Nygren is also questioned, particularly by those who regard the historic-genetic approach to history the more scientific method for investigating religious ideas. Is not motif research a synthetic method rather than an analytic one? Is it not built on philosophical intuition rather than on scientific investigation? Again, Nygren's answer can be summarized in a few succinct points: (1) Basic motifs are not subjective or arbitrary judgments, but represent instead historically given fundamental idea structures that are objectively present as the unifying core within each particular type of faith. (2) Although basic motifs may be intuitively discerned to begin with, the intuitions serve only in the way of working hypotheses which are subsequently verified by reference to the material and by way of objective research procedures. (3) The method of verification is clearly intersubjective; motif research is always open to testing, that is, by reference to the greater or lesser resistance or pliancy of the material relative to the interpretive hypothesis. (4) Motif research never claims absoluteness or finality for its views, but remains always tentative, always relative, subject to challenge and correction, and open to further research. (5) The method of motif research is clearly the most objective scientific approach to the determination of the uniqueness of historical faith.

But again Nygren is questioned, and now by theological colleagues who consider the relativity and tentativeness of motif research its most serious weakness. Can the tentative results of scientific motif research serve as starting point for dogmatic theology? Must not Christian systematic theology make unconditional claims to validity, and must it not therefore be built on a secure and stable basis? Nygren's answer is simple; it can be summarized in the following points: (1) Faith, or faith-reflection, and the scientific study of faith are two different things; the first represents the truth of faith, the second seeks only to give a true account of the faith it studies. (2) As these represent two categorically different thought-forms, the qualities of the one are not applicable to the other. (3) Faith represents an absolute commitment on the part of the believer, and faith-reflection is therefore characterized by certainty and stability. (4) The scientific study of faith—scientific systematic theology—is of necessity subject to the conditions under which all science operates, and is therefore relative. (5) In the total complex of religious understanding, there is room both for the autonomous unconditionality of faith-reflection and for the scientific tentativeness of historical-critical systematic theology.

If, finally, we should ourselves want to know exactly how motif research operates in practice, Nygren has given a clear account, both of the way the theologian asks his questions and of the way he seeks his answers. In the following section of this book we shall give attention to some examples of motif research in Nygren's own works. Here, we shall close our analysis of Nygren's theological methodology by focusing on its most crucial point: the actual formulation of "the question of a categorical nature" which the systematic theologian asks and in terms of which he interprets his material.

The process includes three identifiable steps: First, there is the general, categorical question, "the question of the eternal"; then, there is the question concerning the existential qualities of the experience of the eternal, "the question of revelation, judgment, reconciliation, and fellowship"; and finally, there is the direct question concerning the essential nature of the particular faith that is studied, "the question of the fundamental motif." Motif research can of course ask its question on any one of these levels. But Nygren emphasizes that only when the theologian comes to raise the direct question concerning the fundamental motif of the faith he studies does he have the possibility of reaching a full and detailed understanding of his material.

All religion represents a relationship to the eternal. But if the systematic theologian approaches his material on the basis of *the general categorical question,* he will only find himself confronted with a series of different conceptions of the eternal. In the case of Christianity, the eternal is of course God. Christianity is thus distinguished from other religions by being a theistic, theocentric faith. But the theologian will want to know more. He will want to know how the relationship with the eternal is experienced; what are its existential dimensions or its spiritual qualities. So he raises *the existential question.* He then becomes aware of another level of meaning in his material and another set of differences between various types of faith. Every religion experiences the eternal in terms of revelation, judgment, reconciliation, and fellowship. In the case of Christianity, all these dimensions in the experience of the eternal are mediated through Christ. Christianity thus distinguishes itself from all other religions by having a personal, "Christocentric" focal point. But the theologian will still want to know more. He will want to know precisely how the relationship with the eternal, mediated through an existential focal point, is structured; what its essential nature and meaning is. And so he raises *the question of the fundamental motif.* With this he is finally on his way to identifying the systematic center and core of the faith he studies. All types of faith have a central motif. In the case of Christianity, says Nygren, the systematic center is God's *agape.* Christianity is distinguished from all other faiths by the fact that here absolutely everything is determined by the unlimited, unqualified, unending nature of God's own love.

With this, we have arrived at another threshold in Nygren's thought—the transition between his methodological principles and his theological work. Nygren has set out to define an approach to theology which is marked by scientific objectivity and doctrinal essentiality. With the analysis of Nygren's attempt to establish the scientific respectability of systematic theology now completed, we can turn our attention next to the way Nygren interprets Christian essence.

Part Four

IN SEARCH OF CHRISTIAN ESSENCE

IX. The Permanent Element

When Anders Nygren started his theological career in the early decades of this century, the champions of theology were faced with serious challenges from several corners. Not only were they confronted by increasing numbers of aggressive opponents among philosophers and scientists; they were challenged also by a number of colleagues in their own camp who insisted that theology had gone wrong and needed to be reoriented to the modern age. In 1912, the year Nygren received his first theological degree, the world of theology was still in shock from the impact of two solid punches, one to the heart, the other to the head. The blows had been administered partly by the publication of Adolf von Harnack's famous book *What is Christianity?* and partly by Albert Schweitzer's great work *The Quest for the Historical Jesus.* Harnack's book amounted to a demand for the bankruptcy of dogmatic theology; Schweitzer's served to focus attention on the insolvency of biblical scholarship. It was not a very pleasant time to start a theological career.

Even so, Nygren decided to get into the ring. He was anxious to see theology hold its own against the onslaughts of outside opponents, and he was eager to do theology in such a way as to prove its continued viability in the face of radical questioning from within. His aim became a twofold one: to establish dogmatics or systematic theology as a respectable scientific discipline, and to relate theology to Christian life and faith in a responsive and responsible manner. Nygren spent roughly the first ten years of his career pursuing the first goal; then, during the late 1920s and early 1930s, he began to give attention to the second.

We have already described how Nygren went about establishing the scientific respectability of systematic theology. We must now shift our focus and attempt to understand what is involved in his pursuit of Christian essence.

We cannot, of course, hope to cover every aspect of Nygren's theology here—that would require investigations far more detailed than could be accommodated within the pages of this book. It would also involve the development of a systematic structure far more elaborate than Nygren himself has produced. What we can do is to observe three characteristic emphases in Nygren's exposition of Christian faith—his analysis of "the permanent element of Christianity," his investigations concerning "the central motif of Christianity," and his interpretation of "the key symbol of Christianity." These are set forth in three particular works by Nygren, *The Permanent Element in Christianity*, *Agape and Eros*, and *The Atonement as a Work of God*.[1] For Nygren, the permanent element is *Christ;* it is the Christocentricity of Christian faith which constitutes the dynamic core of Christianity and which remains unchanged, regardless of how Christian doctrine has been developed and altered through the centuries. Again, for Nygren, the central motif is *agape;* it is the message of God's own love which is the unifying principle of Christian faith and which determines its content, from the least little detail to the complete system of its kerygma. And thirdly, for Nygren, the key symbol is the *cross;* it is the singular event of the death of Christ which is the fundamental mystery of the Christian message and which must be grasped, if one is ever to reach a responsible understanding of the faith.

We shall look at the first of these emphases in a little more detail here, then go on to the others in subsequent chapters.

THE QUESTION OF PERMANENCE

Nygren starts [2] by affirming the historicity and mutability of Christianity, yet he emphasizes that with all the changes it has undergone through the ages, Christianity persists. Change and permanence are both part of the profile of the faith. Both must be affirmed. To deny the one and affirm the other would lead to little but confusion.

But in order to hold the two together, it is necessary that the perspective be a clear and consistent one. There are those, says Nygren, who resist the idea that Christianity changes. They are convinced that the Christian faith has eternal significance, and that Jesus Christ is the same, yesterday, today, and for all eternity. They cannot think of Christianity without ascribing to it the unchanging character of the eternal. But this, in Nygren's view, rests on categorical confusion. There are two different contexts of meaning involved, one theological, the other historical. God is eternal; he does not change. But Christianity is not eternal; it is historical, and everything historical is subject to change. The two perspectives must not be mixed.

To illustrate how Christianity changes according to the historical situation, Nygren refers to the Apostle Paul, living and working in the first century, in contrast to Luther, set within the cultural context of the sixteenth century. Paul's environment was dominated by Judaism and Hellenism, while Luther's was influenced by the conflicting forces of medieval Catholicism and the Renaissance. To criticize Paul for relating his theology to the Hellenistic culture of his day is really rather naïve. And to interpret Luther as though his reformation activity simply meant the restoration of Christianity in terms of its original meaning is also quite crude. Paul and Luther represented *the renewal of Christianity* for their day and time. As they explicated the faith, much of its traditional dress and coloring were discarded, and since their time, many of their ideas which were historically conditioned have disappeared, even among those who count themselves as Paul's or Luther's closest followers.

Christianity, says Nygren, is rather like a plant which grows by assimilating or assuming into itself all sorts of substances from its environment. A plant preserves its own nature in all circumstances—it remains true to the character of its species. But it is capable of assuming the most varied forms, depending on the soil or the climate or the seasons, as they change. A birch is a birch, whether it is tall and straight or low and gnarled, whether it is in the full green of summer or stands bare and lifeless in winter. That is also how it is with Christianity. Wherever it appears, it bears the marks of its place—the age, the culture, the context within which it is set. Yet it never surrenders its own unique character.

But what is it that persists? What is this character that has remained the same in spite of all the changes which time and circumstance have caused in Christianity through the ages? As Nygren sees it, this question has not been answered correctly in the modern period. Much of the discussion of the relationship between Christianity and culture has been marred by category mixing and logical confusion.

Nygren refers, for example, to the common practice of defining Christianity as a series of beliefs concerning God, the creation and constitution of the world, man, Christ, the end of history—ideas which are then seen to have been challenged, one by one, by the progress of modern science. From this point of view, Christianity is considered a primitive or obsolete sort of science, knowledge which slowly but surely is being replaced as science is updated. Bit by bit the original content of Christian faith is thus being discarded. The only part of it that the modern age still has room for is that diminishing fraction which has not yet been challenged by science or which the believer considers its untouchable core. This last little remnant of the faith is then considered the permanent element of Christianity.

Another approach which also falls under Nygren's criticism

is the attempt to seek refuge from the relativity of history in metaphysics. The distinction between the husk and the kernel of Christianity, between that which is historically conditioned and can be abandoned and that which is eternally valid and therefore permanent, is left in the hands of the philosopher of religion who, it is said, is particularly equipped to separate the valid from the invalid, the absolute from the relative. He, more than anybody, should be able to identify the permanent element of Christianity—that which is untouched by historical changes.

To Nygren's way of looking at it, both of these approaches are quite mistaken, and for two simple reasons: they confuse religion and science and they separate permanence and historicity. Both of Nygren's objections are anchored in his analytical philosophy. The first has its basis in the analysis of the presuppositions of meaning and in Nygren's theory of the logical autonomy of each particular category or context of meaning within human experience. To Nygren, religion is not science, and science not religion. As two entirely different presuppositional contexts, they do not admit of mutual criticism. To think that as science progresses Christianity is forced to retreat is to misunderstand the integrity and autonomy of both science and religion. Nygren's second objection is based on his analysis of the relationship between the universal and the particular and his theory of the radical historicity of religious commitments or faith. In Nygren's view, there is no "eternal religion," only particular historical religions. The essence of religion is not some metaphysical pure and permanent idea, but the historical *grundmotifs* of historical faiths.

As Nygren sees it, the attempt to separate the eternal from the temporal is built on a popular illusion, namely, the idea that the absolute is somehow manifested in history but never identical with it. It is a naïve and thoughtless idea—and equally so whether the revelation of the eternal is thought of in static terms and thus identified with a certain set of unique events of the past or it is considered dynamic and evolutional, something that slowly but surely emerges in the midst of history and will stand out in splendid isolation from everything relative in the end. In either case the eternal is considered objectified in the temporal without being subsumed under the conditions of temporality—an idea which is as illogical on the face of it as it is illegitimate to its core.

How then should the question of the permanent element—the persisting character—of Christianity be raised? Says Nygren, in terms of a historical perspective and by way of objective procedures. Christianity must be approached, first, in full view of the radical historicity of faith, and second, by way of a method that is conducive to an objective investigation of the historical essence of Christian faith. "Radical historicity" means, of course, relativity; "objective investigation procedures" spells motif research.

The historical relativity of Christianity need not, in Nygren's view, be debated. It is a plain fact. Christianity presents itself in history not as a single, standard form of faith but in an endless multiplicity of forms. Anyone with a little knowledge of Christian history knows that Christian faith did not mean the same to Origen as it did to the Apologists, or to Luther as it did to Augustine, or to Francis as it did to Thomas Aquinas. Forms of worship have varied; doctrinal views have changed; ideals of life have evolved. Yet with all this historical relativity, something permanent remains—something abiding, something that is common to all Christians, something that makes Christianity what it is.

But what is it? And how is it to be approached? Nygren's answer represents an interesting application of his principle of historical understanding—that the depth of understanding is correlative with the scope of the context within which the material is considered. To understand the permanent element of Christianity in an objective way one must take a step back from the many different forms of Christianity and raise a more general question, namely, what is the essential nature of religion? Christianity is after all a form of religion. It has emerged in history as a unique answer to the religious question. By considering Christianity from the perspective of the universal religious question, one gains a context in which one can identify its unique character—distinct from all other religious types—without having to consider its many different forms in comparison with one another. The permanent element of Christianity is then understood as the dynamic center of the Christian faith—that which characterizes the Christian religion as a religion, regardless of how Christian faith commitments have otherwise changed and how interpretations of Christian doctrine have otherwise varied throughout history.

But the question of permanence involves one additional dimension, another element of relativity, that must be considered. The Christian religion is not the only form of religion or the only answer to the religious question. The relationship between the various forms of religion is in many ways like the relationship between the various forms of Christianity—no single form of religion can be said to represent religion itself. It is not possible, simply by studying the various religions, separately or in comparison with one another, to determine what is the essence of religion. To identify the essential element in religion it is necessary to take another step back—and now from the many different forms of religion to the roots of religion in the life of the human spirit. Religion is after all a form of spiritual life. It belongs within the spectrum of fundamental human concerns, and it is a distinct context of meaning within human awareness. It is by considering religion from the perspective of the fundamental categories of human awareness that one gains the context within which one can identify the characteristics of religious awareness—essential religiousness—as distinct from all other dimensions of consciousness or contexts of meaning, and without having to take sides among the different forms of religion or allowing one's own convictions to bias one's definition of religious essence.

Nygren has thereby determined his own approach to the question of permanence. He will first analyze the various dimensions of human spiritual life, seeking to identify the essential nature of the religious context of meaning. Next, he will explore the religious experience of man, seeking to identify the existential characteristics of religious awareness. Third, he will examine Christianity as one among the many historical realizations of the religious context of meaning, seeking to identify the unique character of this particular religious type.[3] In Nygren's view, it is precisely that which characterizes Christianity as a religious type that is the permanent element of Christianity.[4]

THE CHARACTER OF CHRISTIANITY

At this point we shall bring into focus the final step in Nygren's examination of Christianity as religious type.[5] We have already observed how Nygren goes about determining the essential nature of the religious context of meaning, and how he analyzes the existential qualities of religious experience.[6] The religious category is the category of the eternal; religious experience is the experience of the revelation of the eternal, the judgment of the eternal, reconciliation with the eternal, and fellowship with the eternal. What characterizes Christianity as religious type is the unique way in which it interprets the existential encounter with the eternal.

The most fundamental distinguishing mark of Christianity, according to Nygren, is that it puts in focus not a certain idea or a certain set of doctrinal affirmations but *a person.* At the center of Christian faith and Christian experience stands *the Christ.* He is the one who puts the distinguishing seal on everything that Christianity stands for. Schleiermacher was entirely correct in saying that "Christianity is essentially distinguished from other faiths by the fact that everything in it is related to the redemption accomplished by Jesus of Nazareth."[7] And Aulén is altogether justified in saying that "it is impossible to separate Christianity from Christ without disrupting it and robbing it of its uniqueness."[8] Says Nygren:

> When we contemplate the innumerable forms of Christianity both past and present, we ask: Is there anything permanent amid all this change? And we can now give our answer in the words of the New Testament: "Jesus Christ is the same yesterday and today, yea for ever" (Hebr. 13:8). He is the permanent element in Christianity; he is the central, the essential thing, the thing which sets its seal upon everything."[9]

As he proceeds to explicate the essential character of Christianity, Nygren argues that in Christianity the *revelation* of the eternal, the *judgment* of the eternal, the *reconciliation* of man with the eternal, and the *fellowship* of man with the eternal are all seen to be manifested in Jesus Christ. This section of Nygren's book *The Permanent Element in Christianity* is in reality an outline of a Christocentric systematic theology, a highly compressed exposition of the essential elements of Christian faith and experience in Christocentric terms.

Important in Nygren's exposition of *the Christian concept of revelation* is that his Christocentricity does not as it has with certain other theologians of the twentieth century develop into sheer Christomonism. Although Nygren does emphasize that in Christ, as nowhere else, the Christian finds the eternal revealed in time, this does not mean that Christ is seen as the only revelation of the eternal, or that all other revelation, natural or historical, is invalidated by the unique revelation of God in Christ. Special revelation, though unique, stands in continuity with general revelation or natural revelation. Nygren is quite clear on that point. But he emphasizes that the continuity of revelation is manifested only in one direction—from God, through Christ, to nature; not from nature, "naturally," via Christ, to God. For Nygren, it is only by having one's eyes opened to the eternal by the revelation in Christ that one can begin to find traces of God's revelation all over creation.

Thus, from the standpoint of systematic theology, one finds Nygren to take a balanced view of revelation. He leaves room for an open and inclusive concept while emphasizing the centrality, even priority, of the revelation in Christ. On a couple of points, however, Nygren is categorical and unbending, namely, when he underscores that the revelation of God, as interpreted in Christianity, is actual and concrete, not speculative or ideological, and when he stresses that Christianity is not truly Christianity where Christ is considered something less than the personal revelation of the eternal God. The first of these points is turned against those whose interpretation of revelation makes it primarily a matter of thought or dogma, and whose concept of revelation is metaphysical, theoretical, and static. Nygren desires to keep religion religious, and the best way to do that is to keep the concept of revelation existential, dramatic, and dynamic. The second point is directed against the attempt to make Christianity a natural religion, whether in terms of generally accepted religious categories or in terms of a universal ethical or aesthetic appeal. Says Nygren, "In cases where the religious question is not a live issue, or where the satisfaction of this need is found elsewhere than in Christ, we ought for the sake of clarity to avoid using the word Christianity." [10] For the Christian, Christ is the personal breakthrough of the eternal in time. Nothing less than that can truly be described as Christian faith.

When we come, second, to Nygren's exposition of *the Christian concept of judgment*—that seriousness or spiritual disquiet which accompanies the confrontation with the eternal—Nygren emphasizes the dramatic heightening of the existential challenge which takes place when we consider ourselves confronted, not merely with an ideal or a rule of law, but with the divine presence itself, with the purity and power of the eternal, or with perfection in human form. When the eternal is thus disclosed among men, it causes an ultimate radicalization of man's sense of unworthiness and sin. It results in the complete transvaluation of all human existence, all worldly values. Christ, the revelation of God, is at the same time the revelation of the truth about man. In the encounter with Christ, *we* are judged, as are all our ideals and values—the entire system of human self-evaluation. The revelation of Christ, far from confirming our natural idealism, is the most radical challenge to all our values. Christianity is not an endorsement of human morality, but the most serious questioning of it. Says Nygren, "To know Christ is to know judgment passed on oneself; to know Christ is to know oneself a miserable sinner." [11]

One should note in this context that when Nygren emphasizes the judgment which is part of the experience of revelation he is closely related to what we might call the element of law (*nomos*) in Christianity. Many of Nygren's critics have charged him with concentrating solely on the agape-motif and ignoring the nomos-motif altogether. This may be true where Nygren has engaged in motif research. He may be charged with having narrowed his perspective too much where he chooses to analyze the interaction between agape and eros and does not in similar fashion analyze the relationship between agape and nomos. But in the present context, where Nygren outlines in a systematic manner the fundamental characteristics of Christian faith, the element of law or judgment is clearly present. And here it is not an addendum, something separate or secondary to the essence of the faith, but integral to it, part of the character of Christian existence, an essential dimension of the God-relationship as the Christian experiences it in Christ. If ever the nomos-motif was considered central to Christian faith and life and consistent with the agape of God in Christ, it is here.

The third part of Nygren's exposition of the essential character of Christianity focuses on *the Christian concept of reconciliation or atonement*, and here Nygren makes no secret of the fact that he considers himself faced with the very essence of Christianity. Once more Christianity is said to be characterized by Christocentricity. It is in Christ that the Christian experiences not only revelation and judgment, but also redemption. The sin which is "discovered" in the revelation of Christ is at the same time "covered" by Christ. This, says Nygren, is the most profound mystery of Christian faith and life—how the eternal, who in coming close to man crushes him with a sense of unworthiness and distance, at the same time restores man by grace and admits him to a new relationship with the eternal, based on forgiveness of sins. Here is the core of Christianity; take this away and there is no longer any Christianity.

Important in Nygren's exposition of the Christian concept of reconciliation is the emphasis that redemption is altogether God's own initiative. The Christocentricity of Christian faith is solidly anchored in theocentricity. The Christian is not allowed to fall into Christolatry. As long as Nygren is talking about revelation and judgment, Christolatry is not a serious problem —Christ is clearly the manifestation of God's self-revelation, not a teacher who on his own initiative manages to spread the knowledge of God. But in the context of reconciliation the idea often emerges that here God is the passive party, to be acted upon; not the active agent but the injured party. Christ is then thought of as man's representative and intermediary who comes on the scene to do an atoning work which is somehow required by God before God will allow sinners to be readmitted to his favor. Nygren wants none of this. As he interprets the atonement, there is a continuity between revelation and reconciliation, between the God who acts to reveal himself in Christ and the God who acts to restore man to himself through Christ. The central paradox of the Christian message is that God, the injured one, himself acts to overcome that which separates man from God. We shall meet these emphases again when we come to analyze Nygren's principal exposition of the atonement in chapter XI.

The fourth and final aspect of Nygren's exposition of essential Christian faith has to do with *the Christian concept of fellowship and union with God.* Again Nygren focuses on the Christocentricity of the Christian God-relationship.

The terms *fellowship* and *God-relationship* are used in various ways by Nygren. At times he uses these terms in a general sense to refer to religious experience as a whole, to the total relationship between God and man, man and God. The terms then include all the facets of religious experience. Nygren has even suggested that "fellowship with God" can function as an alternate formulation of the general category of religion. In the present context, however, Nygren uses these terms in a more limited sense. He is explicating the nature of the new relationship between God and man which is established as a result of reconciliation and atonement, and he indicates that it is entirely different from the relationship which is based on revelation and characterized by a sense of judgment. Fellowship with God, in this context, has a distinctive new quality to it; it represents the new life which the Christian believer has "in Christ," in responsiveness to God's grace, in gratitude and obedience, in self-giving and commitment.

Significantly, Nygren confesses that he finds it impossible to avoid describing the Christian life as characterized by some form of Christ-mysticism. The Christian goes through a radical transition from self-centeredness to Christ-centeredness. In one sense he loses his life but, paradoxically, he is not annihilated as an individual. He finds his life precisely by losing it, namely, in Christ. The Christian is one whose life is not in the self, but in Christ. No longer does he consider himself the center of his own existence; he is, in truth, not his own—he belongs to another. As Paul the apostle expresses it, "It is no longer I who live, but Christ who lives in me" (Gal. 2:20).

THE PERMANENT ELEMENT

Nygren's exposition of the characteristic emphases of Christian faith and life focuses on the centrality of Jesus Christ. Nygren has thereby identified the permanent element of Christianity. What distinguishes Christianity from all other religions in the world is that here the revelation of the eternal, the judgment of the eternal, the reconciliation with the eternal, and the fellowship with the eternal are all found mediated in the life, the work, the death and the message of Jesus Christ.

When this is said, however, it is necessary to clarify what is meant by "Jesus Christ." The phrase is by no means clear. At the time when Nygren wrote his treatise, theologians were in fact deep in disagreement as to the question whether the emphasis should be put on "the historical Jesus" or on "the Christ of faith." The issue was this: Is Christianity oriented to the gospel which Jesus preached or is it oriented to the gospel concerning Christ? Is being a Christian to have the faith of Jesus, or is it to have faith in Christ? Or, expressed as some did at the time, is Jesus himself part of the gospel, or was he simply the first to proclaim it? Which is the real Christ—the Jesus we find in the Gospels or the Christ which we find in the theology of Paul and John?

Nygren gives a very helpful discussion of these points.[12] In regard to the question whether Christianity has its focus in the teachings of Jesus or in the teachings about Christ, his judgment is that the issue is contrived and ought to be dismissed. Only the speculative mind would be engaged in such inquiries. Christianity cannot be compressed within the teachings of Jesus; nor can it be identified solely with the teachings about Christ. Christianity exists where history and faith meet and where fact and interpretation interact. "Jesus" and "Christ" cannot be torn apart. Jesus is the historical fact with which Christianity is connected; Christ is the religious interpretation of this particular historical person. Christianity does not exist if either the historical event or the faithful interpretation is missing. The authenticity of Christian faith can only be expressed in terms of the classical confession, "Jesus is Christ."

Nygren does accept the notion that the New Testament image of Jesus Christ is a complex one and that it is important to sort out what is what in the biblical sources. It must be made clear that the New Testament does not represent a simple recitation of historical facts but that it has attached to these facts a number of interpretations or elaborations of a theological or kerygmatic nature. Christian faith is never interested in Jesus of Nazareth simply as a historical person. What gives Jesus such unique significance is that in him Christian believers have found eternity breaking through on the historical scene. This breakthrough of the eternal is not itself a demonstrable historical fact; rather, it represents the meaning of the life and work of Jesus of Nazareth as seen from the perspective of faith.

But the fact that the New Testament picture of Christ is an interpretation of the life and work of Jesus does not mean that the historical facticity of Jesus of Nazareth can be dismissed and that we can focus solely on the believer's image of the Christ. The two dimensions of the Christian confession belong together: Jesus is Christ. Christianity did not have its beginning simply in the historical appearance of Jesus; as long as he was considered "after the flesh" he was simply a teacher—better than most, to be sure, but still only a teacher. On the other hand, Christianity did not have its origin in the acquisition of a new set of religious ideas, as by the extension of the human intellect toward a clearer or loftier conception of God. The new and extraordinary thing which Christianity represents in the world of religion is the conviction that here, in the confrontation with Jesus of Nazareth, we are confronted with the eternal God. As Nygren says, "The new religion, Christianity, had come into being [only] when the disciples could confess concerning the historical person of Jesus, 'Thou art the Christ, the Son of the living God!' "[13]

So, according to Nygren, the name Jesus Christ is a synthesis of fact and interpretation, history and faith. And so are all the other names used in the New Testament—"Jesus Messiah," "Jesus Son of God," "Jesus Lord," "Jesus Logos." They all represent various attempts to express something of the experience of the early believers—the fact that in this one person, Jesus of Nazareth, they found the revelation of the eternal, the judgment of the eternal, the reconciliation with the eternal, and the new relationship with the eternal.

But this raises one additional question, a historical one: Where did Christianity get its start—with Jesus or with the disciples? As Nygren sees it, regardless of how far back we may go into the history of Christianity we will always find evidence of the type of historical-theological synthesis which the name Jesus Christ represents. This is not only typical of Paul and John; the Synoptic Gospels contain the same kind of statements. Whether Jesus himself actually claimed the title of Messiah or Christ is, of course, a question of considerable historical interest. Nygren recognizes this, but he emphasizes that it is *only* of historical or exegetical interest, and does not bear on the investigation of Christian essence. The absence of the proper sources for determining whether Jesus possessed Messianic self-consciousness does not invalidate the presence of sources which express the Christian confession that Jesus is Christ. Moreover, Christianity does not stand or fall on the issue of its historical beginnings, but on its own essential nature as a faith. And, as Nygren has shown, it is in the essential nature of Christian faith to confess that in Jesus of Nazareth God's Christ has become incarnated among men. Whether Jesus himself believed this can, absurd as it sounds, finally be said to be a question of whether he himself was a Christian. Says Nygren:

> Even if it could be historically proved that Jesus himself did not describe himself as Messiah—a thing which so far has not been made in the least degree credible—or that Jesus himself did not complete this and similar syntheses, even this would be of no significance for our present purposes. We, too, have described these syntheses as religious elaborations. It is more or less irrelevant for our purposes whether Jesus himself gave his disciples the lead in this religious elaboration, or whether he left it to themselves. It is irrelevant because we have seen that the elaboration is necessary to the essence of Christianity; and we have seen that it is only intended to give expression to what is already implicit in that essence.[14]

Nygren's essay *The Permanent Element in Christianity* was first published in 1922. That was a full thirty years before the debate over Christology that centered around Rudolf Bultmann's investigations into New Testament proclamation and mythology. Nygren did not engage himself in that later debate, but his viewpoints were clearly relevant to the issues. In his well-balanced and reasonable manner, Nygren had argued both for the importance of history as history and for the significance of faith as faith. Had the theologians listened, they could have avoided many of the excesses and most of the confusion which typified the so-called demythologization debate. Those who did listen found themselves guided by a steady light toward an enlightened understanding of the essential nature and enduring character of Christian faith.

X. The Central Motif

No churchman who has been anywhere near awake during sermons for the last forty years or so can have missed hearing—at least once from every preacher—an exposition of the difference between *eros*, *philia*, and *agape*, the three Greek terms for love. It has become a favorite way for seminary-educated preachers to exhibit the practical relevance of their theological education and prove the positive value of historical-critical biblical exegesis—and at the same time clarify how the Christian understanding of things differs from the popular notions of men. Most of us nowadays consider the point made. That was not so forty to fifty years ago. At that time, not only did preachers and theologians frequently miss the finer distinctions in the Christian concept of love; the centrality of love in the structure of Christian faith and life was itself often obscured.

It was Anders Nygren's major contribution to the recovery of Christian theology in the twentieth century that he brought this point to the attention of the theological community. He did not invent the agape-motif—a scientific systematic theologian does not, as he says, invent anything new. He only investigates what is there in the traditions of faith which he studies. When he sets it forth, it is not as if it were his own creation. It belongs to the tradition. It is common property. What Nygren did was to focus the attention of the theological community on the centrality of agape in Christian faith and life and explicate the unique qualities of the divine agape, and for this he has received appropriate recognition—it is, in fact, for most people the main thing Nygren is recognized for. All his other contributions, in philosophy, in philosophy of religion, in theological methodology, in theology, or in ecumenical contexts, have to a large extent been overshadowed by his research into the central motif of Christianity.

Nygren may himself have contributed to this concentration of his readers' attention on the investigation of the agape-motif. In the preface to the first edition of *Agape and Eros*, published in 1930, Nygren invited those readers who have no interest in the abstract delineations of methodological principles which are contained in the introductory chapter to skip it and go directly to the first part of the book, where the two conflicting motifs are contrasted. Many of his readers seem to have done just that, thereby missing one of Nygren's most cogent expositions of the unique methodological framework within which he operates. If they had read the introduction—even if it was the only work by Nygren they had ever read—they would have understood that Nygren's investigations of the Christian concept of agape are part of a larger theological enterprise, related to a unique conception of the discipline of systematic theology and to a method which is equally unique in that it combines the concern for scientific objectivity and Christian essentiality within a single methodological principle. By ignoring the introduction, on Nygren's own invitation, many of his readers have missed what Nygren calls "the systematic placement of the problem [of agape] in the larger [theological] context,"[1] and this in turn means that they have tended to miss the real intentions behind Nygren's inquiry into the agape-motif as he himself has declared them.

Nygren has often been criticized for pressing all of Christian theology into a single idea or concept, namely, love. The criticism is groundless. Our exposition of Nygren's views of the permanent element of Christianity has proven the error of this criticism. Nygren does not claim that his study of *eros* and *agape* is a full systematic analysis of the structure and content of Christian doctrine, or that he has covered every conceivable aspect of the agape-motif. He has simply chosen one problem, a complex of issues that is of particular importance to him, namely the interaction between the biblical, evangelical understanding of love and the Greek, Platonic understanding of love. In setting what he considers to be the essential Christian concept of agape in direct confrontation with the conceptions of eros that are characteristic of Greek thought, Nygren hopes to show that the two are representative of basically different types of religion and that Christian theology is in danger of compromising its character when it fraternizes with Greece.

Only if one ignores Nygren's careful analysis of the nature of motif research, only if one disregards Nygren's own understanding of religious motifs, and only if one misinterprets what Nygren is doing in *Agape and Eros,* is it possible to think that Nygren has reduced Christian theology to a single point. But that is not to understand Nygren on the basis of his own presuppositions; it is to misrepresent his views and interpret them clear out of context. No theologian is given his due under such circumstances.

In order to set Nygren's exposition of the agape-motif in its proper context, we shall begin here by observing what he himself says about the whole endeavor.

THE QUESTION OF GRUNDMOTIV

Nygren begins by explaining the twofold task which he has set for himself in *Agape and Eros;* (1) to make a contribution to the understanding of the Christian concept of love, and (2) to illustrate by reference to some important periods of transition the changes and developments that it has undergone in the course of history. The specific aim is to identify the authentic character and essential meaning of the Christian concept of love, and Nygren's approach is that of historical-systematic structural analysis or motif research.

Nygren explains that his main concern in investigating the Christian concept of love has to do with its centrality in the structure of Christian faith and life. It is not the only thing that is characteristic of Christianity, but it is clearly of fundamental importance in any attempt to determine the essential character of Christian faith. It has the function of a *grundmotiv*, a basic motif.

Nygren has thereby established the connection between his investigations of agape and the basic methodological principles which he has developed. *Agape and Eros* is precisely the kind of objective investigation of a historical-empirical religious type which Nygren has identified as "scientific systematic theology." The concept *grundmotiv* also connects the endeavor with the critical analysis of the religious category which Nygren has identified as the task of philosophy of religion. A *grundmotiv*, as Nygren defines it, is "the answer that a particular religious type or faith gives in response to a question of such a fundamental nature as to be considered categorical."[2] The inquiry into the essential content and historical development of the agape-motif is thus related to the two basic presuppositional contexts within which, in Nygren's view, any historical faith or religious type must be understood, namely, the "category context" (the fundamental religious question) and the "motif context" (the particular religious answer).

According to Nygren, when the categorical religious question —the question of the eternal—is raised, the Christian faith answers that the eternal is God and that God is love, agape. Agape is thus *the Christian grundmotiv par preference.* It puts its mark on everything the Christian faith contains; it is the distinguishing characteristic of Christianity—the Christian religions' most original and fundamental concept.

But Christianity has not at all points in its development been equally faithful to this original and fundamental motif. From time to time the Christian *grundmotiv* has been in contention with, and under the influence of, other such fundamental motifs —particularly that which is identified as the Platonic eros-motif. In principle the agape-motif and the eros-motif have nothing to do with one another; they represent two entirely different conceptions of religion—two altogether different religions. But in practice they have come to be closely related, partly because they are both, after all, concepts of love, and partly because they have both played a significant role in the formation of Western culture and Western theology. It is this interaction between the agape-motif and the eros-motif that necessitates the second task which Nygren sets for himself—the analysis of the changes and development which the Christian *grundmotiv* has undergone as a result of the confrontation with Platonic thought. As Nygren sees it, the investigation of the central motif of Christianity must at the same time be a critique of certain crucial periods in the historical development of Christian theology; the analysis of agape must involve a determination of its relationship to eros.

We have now identified the purposes of Nygren's inquiry and the perimeters within which his work on agape and eros must be placed. What Nygren is engaged in is motif research pure and simple—nothing more, nothing less. Nygren is attempting to identify the most essential and characteristic idea of Christian faith, and in the process he finds that he must make clear how this central motif is related to one alternate *grundmotiv* that has been influential on, and in fact at times confused with, the Christian *grundmotiv*. It is all a question of sorting out the relationship between the Christian concept of love and its closest competitor on the Western scene, the Platonic eros.

Nygren's book *Agape and Eros* is an impressively compact presentation of a vast and complicated material. Nygren goes about his task in four distinct steps: He first analyzes the Christian agape-motif in its original purity; next he does the same with the Platonic eros-motif; he then, thirdly, sets the two motifs in direct opposition to one another; and finally he tells the story of the historical struggle between the two motifs, from the time of the early Christian fathers through the Protestant Reformation. We shall not at this point attempt to follow Nygren through every stage of his investigation. Our interest here is primarily to get the feel for the way he defines the central motif of the Christian faith. In the following we shall therefore concentrate on the first major chapter in *Agape and Eros* which is entitled "The *Agape*-Motif." Here is set forth in crystallized form the essential nature of agape as it is expressed in the New Testament, particularly in the message of Jesus and in the Christology of Paul.

AGAPE AND THE NEW GOD-RELATIONSHIP

The first, most fundamental emphasis in Nygren's exposition of the Christian concept of love is focused on the theocentric character of agape. What sets Christianity apart from all other types of religion is the fact that the Christian faith centers around God's own love, not man's. With this is paired Nygren's second emphasis, namely, that the Christian understanding of God's love is not primarily a theoretical or conceptual idea; it is the expression of something much more fundamental, something central to religious life itself, namely, the revelation of a radically new relationship between God and man.

Nygren is here considering the message of Jesus as it is set forth in the Synoptic Gospels, and "radically new" reflects therefore primarily the relationship between the message of Jesus and the roots from which it sprang historically, that is, Judaism. As Nygren sees it, this relationship is marked both by continuity and discontinuity. That there is a certain continuity between Judaism and Jesus' message can be observed in the fact that the commandment to love God and neighbor has a central place in both contexts. But that Jesus' message is basically discontinuous with Judaism becomes evident when one observes how the commandment to love is placed within the structure of the God-relationship as this is interpreted in these different contexts. The difference comes perhaps to clearest expression in Jesus' words, "I came not to call the righteous, but sinners" (Mark 2:17). This statement is a key, says Nygren, both to the understanding of Judaism and to the central motif of Christianity. In Judaism the God-relationship is based on the principle of righteousness and reward. The center around which everything revolves is the law. God's relationship to man is determined by the law; man's relationship to God is likewise determined by the law. The law is the expression of God's will; obedience to the law is the expression of man's faith. The relationship is one of justice. In Christianity, on the other hand, this entire system is terminated. The God-relationship is based on divine grace and forgiveness of sins. God relates to man in terms of love, not law; and love includes even the unrighteous, the unworthy, the sinner. Man is brought into relationship with God, not on the basis of any quality in himself, but solely on the basis of God's unrestricted, unqualified and unlimited agape.

One should observe that Nygren does not make the mistake of ignoring the strong note of grace and love which lies behind the divine covenant, and even the law, in Judaism. He emphasizes, however, that the motif context—the Judaic concept of the God-relationship itself—is so structured as to place love and grace within the requirements of covenant and law, and therefore within a system of retributive justice. From this love and grace the sinner, the unrighteous, is excluded, on principle. That is the principal distinction between the Judaic conception of divine love and the Christian understanding of God's agape. In Christianity, there is an entirely new motif context at work, a God-relationship which is so structured as to include the sinner and give the righteous no preference. Righteous and sinners are all included, not because the righteous are lovable or sinners are somehow preferred, but simply because of the qualities of God's own love. Why does God love? Says Nygren, because his nature is love.

Against the background of the new God-relationship which is set forth in the message of Jesus, Nygren proceeds to offer a preliminary definition of the nature of agape. He focuses on four specific qualities:

1. *Agape is spontaneous and unmotivated.* By this he means that the divine agape does not have its cause or foundation any-

where else than in God's own nature. It is not called forth by any quality in man. Agape is not a judgment regarding man's nature but an expression of God's nature; it is not determined by the character of its object but solely by the character of the subject.

2. *Agape is indifferent to value.* For Nygren it is important to emphasize that when agape includes the sinner, this does not represent a simple inversion of values. It is not as though sinners were somehow more lovable than the righteous. Agape is much more radical than that—it excludes any thought of the value of the object, whether righteous or sinner. There is no evaluation involved at all. Agape overlooks all distinctions of value.

3. *Agape is creative of value.* This, to Nygren, identifies it as *divine* love. God loves not because something is of value to him; on the contrary, that which he loves, in itself nothing, is given worth by being the object of his love. Agape does not simply confirm worth; it creates worth. Agape is a value-creating principle. There is no room in Christian theology for the idea of "the infinite worth of the human soul" as the cause of God's love of man; it is the fact that God loves man that is the cause of any human worth or value.

4. *Agape establishes fellowship.* To Nygren, this means that agape is not only the element which determines the structure of God-relationship, it is the very foundation of the God-relationship itself. There is no other basis on which God relates to man—not righteousness, not repentance, not even faith. There is no way that leads from man to God. The God-relationship is entirely of God's own making, a consequence of God's own *agape;* it is God's own way to man.[3]

But when Nygren has thus explicated the radical theocentricity of the Christian God-relationship and the unique qualities of the divine agape, he is faced next with the task of placing within this context the commandment to love God and neighbor which is continued as a central emphasis in the new covenant of grace as it was in the old covenant of law. The question he is faced with is this: What room is there within a God-relationship which is entirely determined by God's love for man for a commandment that man is to love God and neighbor? As Nygren sees it, this question bears primarily on the qualities of the Christian ethos, and the answer is that in his own life in relation to God and neighbor the Christian is commanded to model himself on the divine agape. The Christian's love of God and neighbor is to be as spontaneous and unmotivated, free of calculation, limitless and unconditional as is the divine agape itself.

There is a difficulty, of course, in speaking of a commandment to love God where love is in principle a spontaneous and unmotivated thing. Is not our love of God always a response to God's love of us, and is it not therefore always motivated by God's agape toward us?

Nygren has here introduced an issue which—as he will show in the subsequent phases of his investigation—has caused considerable difficulties throughout the history of Christian thought. He indicates, however, that in the original testimonies to Jesus' message in the Synoptic Gospels the difficulty does not appear great. The reason is that for Jesus the love of God meant simply "to belong in absolute dedication to God." This belonging or total dedication to God gives the love of God an entirely different quality than that which characterizes qualified or motivated love; it both excludes and includes the spontaneity of human love. It *excludes* it in the sense that it is only by a divine initiative that man is brought into relationship with God; but it *includes* it in the sense that in loving God to whom we belong, we do not seek to gain anything by love. Our love of God is a free, spontaneous dedication to God—a commitment which excludes all egocentric motivations whatever. As Nygren says, God gives his own love for free; man's love of God cannot therefore gain him anything that he does not already have.[4] If our love of God is motivated by anything, the motivation is purely deontological —of the nature of dedication—never teleological, of the nature of seeking love. The Christian's love of God is responsiveness and obedience without thought of reward.

But what of the commandment to love our neighbor? Can it

be similarly incorporated into the agape context? Nygren answers in the affirmative, but he does see certain difficulties. One difficulty is that the commandment to love the neighbor is easily torn loose from its religious or theocentric anchoring. It is seen as something over and beyond the response to God—as some horizontal relationship which the Christian must establish with his neighbor in addition to the vertical relationship of love which he has to God. Nygren rejects this as a clear distortion of Christian love. The Christian's love of neighbor springs from the same roots as his love of God, namely, from the God-relationship which is established by God's agape. The love of neighbor is therefore a spontaneous reflection of that love which the believer has himself experienced in relation to God.

Another difficulty which Nygren considers is that the two commandments to love God and neighbor are often brought together and made into one. This is based on the thought that the only legitimate love for the Christian is the love of God. The love of neighbor is then interpreted not as love of the actual neighbor but of God. Again Nygren rejects what he considers a clear distortion of Christian love. Love of neighbor must mean love of *neighbor*. To say that love of neighbor must be directed not to the neighbor but to "God in the neighbor" is nothing but a return to the concept of a qualified or motivated love. As Nygren sees it, the Christian's love of neighbor must be in the nature of agape. And to assure that the love of neighbor is spontaneous and unmotivated, it is necessary that the neighbor be considered just that—neighbor, fellow man, nothing more, nothing less.

We must note that Nygren does not include the love of self as a legitimate form of Christian love. There is no third part of the commandment to love which requires or legitimizes self-love. In Nygren's view, the idea of self-love has its roots in an altogether different soil than that of the Christian tradition. From the Christian point of view, self-love is the root of sin, the mark of our fallenness and disobedience—man's natural condition. But does not the commandment to love neighbor explicitly state that we also are to love ourselves? No, says Nygren, quite the contrary. It explicitly excludes self-love. The commandment says that just as by nature we love ourselves, we shall now, under the commandment and in obedience to God, love the neighbor. Christian love is thereby given a new direction—away from the self and toward the neighbor.[5]

Nygren has a particularly interesting interpretation of the emphasis in Jesus' message on the love of enemy. He does not consider it a separate commandment but an essential part of the commandment to love neighbor. By separating love of enemy from the love of neighbor, one is only showing that one has not understood the nature of agape. In fact, by considering the love of enemy a radical intensification of the love of neighbor, one is showing that one has not grasped the meaning of agape. Love of neighbor is in its essence the love of enemy, for if love has the qualities of agape—spontaneity, nonmotivation—it is irrelevant whether the neighbor is a friend or an enemy. It is in the very nature of agape to love the unlovable; God's agape is the love of sinners, the Christian's agape is the love of enemy.

AGAPE AND THE CROSS

In all of Nygren's explorations of the original meaning of agape as this is set forth in the New Testament, the theology of Paul clearly plays a central role. In fact, Nygren considers Paul's theology the best possible exposition of the innermost intentions of Jesus' message.

In this, Nygren places himself in direct opposition to theologians like Harnack and Wrede who insisted on drawing a sharp line of demarcation between Jesus and Paul. In their opinion, Jesus' message was simple, Paul's, complex; Jesus' gospel was concerned with the kingdom of God, Paul's, with Christology; Jesus' preaching was primarily ethical, Paul's, dogmatic; Jesus' thought was anchored in Judaism, Paul's, in Hellenism. Paul is therefore considered the second founder of Christianity; he is said to have made of Christianity something it was not intended to be by the first founder, Jesus.

In contradicting Harnack and Wrede, Nygren does not deny the fact that the writings of Paul belong within a conceptual world entirely different from that which meets us in the Synoptic Gospels. But this, in Nygren's view, is not sufficient grounds for charging that Paul's message is different from that of Jesus or that the essential meaning of the faith has been changed. The way to determine whether there is continuity or discontinuity in the relationship between Jesus and Paul is to go back to the central motif of Jesus' message and see whether this is still intact in the theology of Paul. Nygren proposes, in fact, that the investigation of the agape-motif in Paul's theology can make an important contribution not only to the understanding of agape but to the clarification of the question concerning the relationship of Paul to Jesus, as well.

Paul's theology is usually interpreted against the background of his religious experience—particularly the dramatic conversion on the road to Damascus. Nygren follows the same procedure. The heart of the Damascus experience is that here Saul the persecutor became Paul the apostle. It was a radical transition. In this experience Paul discovered both an entirely new kind of God-relationship, unlike his earlier conception of faith, and a new understanding of the nature of the divine agape on which the new God-relationship is based and through which it was realized in his own experience. Before this, Paul had understood the God-relationship as having its center in the law; he had thought himself acceptable to God because of his dedication to the strictest possible observation of the requirements of piety and his own righteousness in the face of the law. Now, however, Paul realized that his own pursuit of righteousness before the law had brought him to sin in the highest potential—to the ultimate disobedience of fighting against God's own work in the world. His own righteousness, far from leading him closer to God, had actually led him into enmity with God. Yet in the very moment of Paul's greatest sin, God took the initiative to come to him, confront him in love, and—miracle of miracles—call him to be an apostle! As Nygren interprets it, Paul's conversion was not from sin to righteousness, but from righteousness to agape—from a God-relationship based on his own pursuit of God to a God-relationship based on God's pursuit of man—or from egocentricity to theocentricity. Paul discovered that human righteousness is not a way to God at all. The only basis for God-relationship is God's own way to man, agape.

To Nygren's mind, this is all entirely continuous with Jesus' own message. Yet he recognizes that Paul's conception of agape is not simply taken over from Jesus. It represents a further development and expansion of Jesus' message, and in two specific ways: Paul is the one who begins to use agape as the technical term for the new God-relationship revealed in Christ; he is also the one who sets the concept of agape in direct relation to the central event of the Christian kerygma, namely, the cross. In both these ways Paul can be said to go beyond the elements of theology which were expressed in Jesus' preaching as this is described in the Synoptic traditions, but in doing so he did not break the continuity between himself and the originator of the faith, and he did not make the gospel any less accessible or understandable, as Harnack and Wrede had claimed. On the contrary, Paul's extensive use of the concept agape, and his interpretation of the cross of Christ as the central symbol of divine love, are entirely consistent with the new God-relationship which is proclaimed by Jesus and with the exposition of the nature of God's agape which is contained in the Synoptic Gospels.

Nygren's interpretation of Paul's *theologia crusis* is a remarkably lucid summary of Christian soteriology as seen in the light of agape. He shows that for Paul the cross of Christ and the agape of God are close corollaries. The cross, which for Paul is the focal point of the new God-relationship, can only be understood in the light of agape; and correspondingly the essential nature of God's agape can only be understood in the light of the cross. As Paul develops it, the Christian concept of love is uniquely "the agape of the cross."

Nygren bases this interpretation of Paul on what he calls "the classical expression of the *agape* of the cross," Romans 5:6–10 (RSV):

> While we were yet helpless, at the right time Christ died for the ungodly. Why, one will hardly die for a righteous man—though perhaps for a good man one will dare even to die. But God shows his love for us in that while we were yet sinners Christ died for us. Since, therefore, we are now justified by his blood, much more shall we be saved by him from the wrath of God. For if while we were enemies we were reconciled to God by the death of his Son, much more, now that we are reconciled, shall we be saved by his life.

From this, Nygren draws the following specific points:

1. Paul centers his understanding of agape on the cross. By so doing he has put the capstone on the biblical interpretation of agape. No other expression of God's agape is as explicit in regard to the nature and meaning of agape as is the cross. The cross says that God's agape is self-giving, self-sacrificing love—love that sacrifices to the uttermost.

2. The agape which is revealed in the death of Christ is not something separate from God's love; God is himself the acting agent in the cross. The agape of Christ is the agape of God; to the Christian, agape is uniquely "God's agape in Christ Jesus" (Rom. 8:39). In the death of Christ, God himself reconciled the world to himself (2 Cor. 5:19). It was all "from God." The cross is agape's way to man's salvation.

3. Never has the spontaneous and unmotivated nature of agape been as clearly revealed as in the death of Christ. To give one's life for the righteous or the worthy—that would be motivation! But to give one's life for the weak, the ungodly, sinners, God's enemies—that is spontaneous grace! *Grace* and *agape* are therefore, for Paul, synonymous terms.

4. The clearest possible expression of the nature of God's agape is that it includes not only sinners but the ungodly, God's enemies. This is the secret which God has only now revealed, in the new covenant, namely, that his love and grace know no bounds or limits. This is the message that God has given Paul to proclaim. Paul does not consider his interpretation of "the agape of the cross" his own free creation; to his mind, the agape

of the cross is not an idea but a reality. It is the dramatic demonstration of the love of God on behalf of those who are fallen and estranged.

Having shown the continuity between Paul's *theologia crusis* and Jesus' proclamation of the new God-relationship, Nygren proceeds to analyze Paul's interpretation of the commandment to love God and neighbor. Paul's interpretation of the agape of the cross focuses, of course, primarily on God's own agape, but there are indications that Paul is also concerned with the Christian's agape, that love which is "the fulfilling of the law" (Rom. 13:10).

Once more Nygren finds Paul to be entirely consistent with the message of Jesus as this is presented in the Synoptic tradition. But there is one difference: Paul is not as emphatic in regard to the commandment to love God as he is in regard to the love of neighbor. For him, it is the love of neighbor which is most uniquely the fulfillment of the law. This fact has often been noted by biblical theologians, and it has become a problem in the interpretation of Paul. It has been suggested, for example, that Paul here seems to have slipped from the explicitly religious anchoring of the Christian ethos which is expressed in the close correlation between the love of God and the love of neighbor. Nygren rejects this view. It is not the combination of the love of God and the love of neighbor that guarantees the religious anchoring of the Christian ethos, *but the close connection between God's agape and our love of neighbor.*

In regard to the commandment to love God, Nygren finds that the reason Paul is disinclined to use the term agape in such contexts is that our love of God is not in its nature entirely spontaneous and unmotivated, the way agape is. Instead, it is conditioned by God's agape toward us—prevenient agape—and represents, therefore, an *answering* love, a reflection of God's own love. Within the context of the God-relationship, which for Paul is determined entirely by the qualities of God's agape, Paul therefore chooses a different term when he speaks of man's response, namely, faith (*pistis*). In this way, says Nygren, Paul has overcome the problem which attaches to the Synoptic tradition of how to reconcile the spontaneous and unmotivated character of agape with the responsive and conditioned character of our relationship to God.

Nygren finds that Paul's problem returns with full force, however, in the context of the commandment to love neighbor. If agape is so entirely spontaneous and unmotivated as God's own love is, how can Paul use this term for the Christian's love of neighbor, which cannot—at least not in the same sense—be altogether spontaneous and unmotivated?

The answer, says Nygren, is that Paul anchors the Christian ethos not in man's own love but in the agape of God—or the agape of Christ—working in and through us. In relation to the neighbor, the Christian is not himself the subject, the lover; God, Christ, the Spirit of God, the Spirit of Christ, agape itself is! Says Paul, "It is no longer I who live, but Christ who lives in me" (Gal. 2:20). It is God's own agape which "has been poured into our hearts through the Holy Spirit which has been given to us" (Rom. 5:5). So it is *God's agape* which is the substance of the Christian's life; he himself has nothing to give. The Christian's love of neighbor is not his own love, but God's. For Paul, both the Christian faith and the Christian ethos are thus entirely theocentric in orientation, and in this, says Nygren, Paul is in full and complete harmony with the intentions of Jesus' message.

We must break off the summary of Nygren's great work *Agape and Eros* at this point. Our purpose, insofar as the present chapter is concerned, is accomplished. We have seen how Nygren explicates the central motif of Christianity, and with it his interpretation of the essential character of Christian faith and life. Seldom has any theologian managed to identify that one thought, that unique experience, that single reality which gives Christianity its essential character and meaning with greater clarity and logical consistency than has Anders Nygren. Whatever else he has contributed to the recovery of authentic Christian theology in the twentieth century, this must undoubtedly rank as his most shining accomplishment.

XI. The Key Symbol

No single facet of doctrine has engaged the leading theologians of Sweden to a greater degree than has the doctrine of the atonement. Billing wrote a major work on it; Aulén has contributed a brilliant study of the "classical-dramatic" interpretation of the atonement; Bring has written extensively on the subject.[1] With his own theological interests focused so clearly on the essential character and central motifs of Christian faith, it was only natural that Anders Nygren should also come to be engaged by this doctrine. As we have seen, in Nygren's view the permanent element in Christianity is Christ, the central motif agape—and agape, most uniquely, the agape of the cross. To understand Christianity at all, it is necessary to understand the key symbol of the Christian kerygma, the atoning death of Christ. It is from here the lines go out to every part of the Christian system of beliefs, determining the interpretation of God's word and work, as a whole and in detail. As Nygren says:

> The thought of atonement, which is of fundamental importance for all religion, is in a quite special sense the central issue for Christianity, inasmuch as the message of the Cross of Christ contains the whole of Christianity.[2]

Nygren's essay on the atonement, first published in 1932, was entitled *Försoningen en gudsgärning.*[3] Designed as a study book for the Christian Student Movement, it is short and simple, yet its content is pregnant. Nygren takes as his starting point the Pauline text from 2 Corinthians, 5:18–19: "All this is from God, who through Christ reconciled us to himself and gave us the ministry of reconciliation; that is, God was in Christ reconciling the world to himself. . . ."

The text undergirds an explicitly theocentric point of view, and Nygren makes clear that he considers this perspective best suited to bringing into view the essential nature of atonement and to overcoming some of the difficulties which the doctrine has caused Christian theologians in the past.

THE QUESTION OF ATONEMENT

Nygren begins by pointing out how central the question of atonement is to religious life: "The meaning of religion is fellowship with God. All real, living religion aims ultimately at a life together of God and man."[4] Atonement has to do with the very essence of religion—what makes religion religious, what makes fellowship with God possible.

The point is simple but basic to Nygren's perspective. He is concerned first of all that theology be interpreted in terms of its religious meaning and not by way of metaphysical speculation. The discussion of religious questions, he says, too easily slips out of the context of religious life and into the realm of intellectualization and theory. Religion is often discussed as a world view, not God-relationship; God is approached as an idea on which one has a certain opinion, not as an ultimate Other with which one has fellowship. It is all theology, of course, and the terminology is often similar. But the language functions within two widely separate worlds of discourse. In the first context the presuppositions are religious ones; in the second, theoretical. As Nygren sees it, the focus on atonement will guarantee that theology stays close to the center of religious life.

But if the atonement is the guarantee that Christian theology is understood from a religious point of view, the orientation on the fellowship character of religion in turn guarantees that the atonement is understood religiously and does not deteriorate into metaphysical speculation. Nygren is emphatic on this point. To approach such religious questions as the atonement on the basis of intellectualistic, metaphysical perspectives has disastrous consequences; the speculative starting point affects, in fact, the interpretation of the atonement more drastically than it does any other doctrine. From the standpoint of metaphysical speculation the whole issue of atonement will, namely, seem superfluous; theoretical inquiries into God's being and nature can well be undertaken without ever seriously raising the question of atonement. The contemplation of God then takes on the character of abstraction—God is conceived merely as an object of thought. From the religious perspective, on the other hand, the situation is entirely different. Here one is concerned precisely with the relationship between God and man, with the establishment of fellowship and communion between the human and the divine. Atonement is therefore the key issue. The doctrine of the atonement is the central doctrine of faith.

Not only is the centrality of atonement guaranteed, from the standpoint of Nygren, in the definition of religion as fellowship; it can be shown to be so with reference to the actual phenomena of human religiosity as well. Wherever man feels himself to be in the presence of God, he has the dual awareness of closeness and distance; he experiences the encounter both as blessedness and judgment. The consciousness of God becomes the consciousness of separation from God. It is here that the idea of atonement has its origins. The relationship between God and man is characterized by the tension between holiness and sin, righteousness and fallenness; atonement is rooted precisely in this tension, and its purpose is the overcoming of it. Says Nygren, the essential meaning of atonement "is the creation of conditions such that God and man can meet each other." [5]

Nygren refers to the history of religion as final proof of the centrality of atonement in the life and thought of religious people. In every religion, at every stage of religiosity, one can find evidence of the quest for atonement—purifications, sacrifices, expiation rituals. As Nygren sees it, to consider these merely as "cultic observances" or "primitive hangovers" is to show little understanding of the essential nature of religion. In all real religion, sacrifices and other means of atonement belong to the heart of the matter. They are precisely what makes fellowship with God possible.

Not all concepts of atonement are equal, however. Nygren draws some rather sharp distinctions, first, between three different pre-Christian or non-Christian approaches to atonement, and second, between these and the Christian approach. They represent, in a way, successive stages in the development of the idea of the atonement, each including an element of criticism of the preceding stage.

The first stage is synonymous with the idea of sacrifice in its original, ordinary sense—as a magically effective rite, an appeasement of the deity's wrath, or as a freely offered gift. Man, who in being confronted with his god becomes conscious of his own unworthiness, seeks to overcome his separation from the deity by offering something that is of value to himself, something that will be desirable in the eyes of his god and that will win for the giver a favorable response—blessings or rewards.

The second stage is reached when man realizes that outward sacrifices are not adequate to reconcile him to his god but must be accompanied by or replaced with a moral commitment or a will to obedience in relation to God's will and command. Reconciliation now appears as a moral attainment. It is not an external act but an internal reorientation—a personal dedication to a life of righteousness. Nygren identifies this stage with the emphases prevalent in the prophetic traditions of the Old Testament and with the dominant intentions in pharisaic piety.

The third stage becomes evident when there is a reaction to moralism and when all of man's obedience, righteousness and love are seen as means of self-exaltation and not as appropriate sacrifices to God at all. In the presence of God the only attitude that befits man is humility—"a broken spirit." It is when a man humbles himself before God and lays aside all pretentions to righteousness or claims to worthiness that the door to salvation and fellowship with God is opened to him. Nygren identifies this as the piety of the "anawim"[6]—"the poor of spirit," "the meek of the earth." It is strongly critical of all pharisaic reliance on work-righteousness.

In comparing Christianity with these pre-Christian notions of atonement, Nygren considers the Christian view at once the fulfillment and the radical abolition of earlier notions of sacrifice. The cross, on the one hand, confirms in the most dramatic way the utter seriousness of the demand for atonement and the truthfulness of the fundamental principle that "there is no fellowship with God without atonement, no atonement without sacrifice."[7] The cross, however, is not to be interpreted as the fourth and final stage in the evolution of man's ideas and procedures concerning sacrificial atonement. It represents, instead, a radically different kind of atonement—atonement as a work of God, not as a work of man. All ideas of human sacrificial atonement have something in common that disqualifies them as means of reconciliation with God, namely, the presumption that something man has or does—whether gifts, righteousness or humility—can be the basis for a right relationship with God. The cross is the final abolition of all such ideas. It says that the atoning sacrifice is God's. Says Nygren,

> Christianity is not the demand for an atonement and reconciliation which man must effect so as to open the way for himself to fellowship with God. Christianity is the word of reconciliation, the message of how God has made a way for himself to us so as to bring us into fellowship with himself.[8]

THEOCENTRIC VERSUS EGOCENTRIC ATONEMENT

Nygren finds that the difference between the pre-Christian ideas of sacrifice and the Christian understanding of atonement is based in a deeper difference, in the understanding of the God-relationship itself. Religion is essentially fellowship with God, a relationship of God and man. But the God-relationship will have an entirely different meaning, depending on where the center of gravity is located—in God or in man. A theocentric God-relationship is diametrically opposed to the egocentric God-relationship.

Egocentricity means quite simply that in every relationship the self and its interests take first priority. Religion in this context becomes something man needs and desires, and God comes into the picture as "the highest good"—that which more than anything else can satisfy man's desires and needs. Theocentricity, on the other hand, means that God is all in all. Even when man is seeking fellowship with God, it is not in order to obtain blessings or rewards of one sort or another, but simply because God's own goodness has taken him captive and compels him to respond.

Nygren sketches the contrast between egocentricity and theocentricity in the following manner:

> In egocentric religion the self stands at the center (1) insofar as the fellowship with God is conceived as serving man's own interests (eudaemonism), and (2) insofar as fellowship with God is thought to be established by man's own actions (moralism). In theocentric religion God stands at the center in both these respects, since (1) what is sought in religion is fellowship with God for his own sake (ethically), and (2) fellowship with God is established by God's own action (evangelically).[9]

In regard to the atonement, specifically, egocentricity starts with man and leads back to man; theocentricity starts with God and leads back to God.

We should note at this point that Nygren does not consider the egocentricity/theocentricity contrast immediately applicable to the comparison of pre-Christian or non-Christian religions and Christian faith. There are tendencies in the theocentric direction in many religions, most notably in the religion of the Old Testament.[10] And there are compromises of the theocentric orientation—accommodations to egocentric interests—in Christian theology at various points in history as well. One such compromise bears on the interpretation of Christ's atoning work and has had a devastating effect on Christian theology for centuries, namely, the idea that it is as a man (*qua homo*) that Christ has made atonement and effectuated reconciliation with God.

The starting point for this interpretation is the conviction that atonement is strictly speaking man's responsibility, and that even when it is interpreted as a divine work atonement must be done through a representative of man and on man's behalf. It is man who has transgressed; it is man, or a representative of man who is capable of doing the work of atonement, who must offer the atoning sacrifice. Behind this interpretation lies a series of assumptions concerning God and the God-relationship which Nygren sees to be diametrically opposed to theocentric Christianity.

The picture is this: High in his heaven God dwells in transcendent holiness; down here, separated from God, man lives the life of a sinner. Without an atonement, neither reconciliation nor fellowship with God can be effectuated. Some change must be accomplished—but by whom? God the Holy One cannot change; the fault is not with him but with man. Surely, one cannot expect God in his holiness to make overtures to sin or adapt himself to the sinner! The change must be effected by man; *he* must be purified and brought into conformity with the will of God. Only when man is conformed to God's holiness can there be any thought of fellowship between God and man.

It is this picture that Nygren describes as a direct contradiction of the Christian message. It is "a slap in the face of everything that is at all central for Christianity," whether one focuses on the incarnation, the life and work of the Christ, or the cross.[11] The incarnation, after all, is the affirmation that God himself has come into the world of sinners—that his holiness did not prevent him from taking the initiative in relation to the unworthy. The life and work of Christ is precisely the proclamation that the Holy One is in the world for the explicit purpose of establishing fellowship with sinners. And what else could possibly be the meaning of Christ's death on the cross than that God has now taken upon himself the work of atonement?

As Nygren sees it, then, Christianity leaves no room whatever for any idea of an atonement or reconciliation that is accomplished by man. "The atonement is from first to last a work of God." [12] The theocentric interpretation creates one difficulty, however. If the atoning work is in any sense a "vicarious sacrifice"—that idea does, after all, have some prevalence in Christian tradition—whose "vicar" or representative is Christ if not ours? And to whom is the sacrifice made if not as a satisfaction or reparation to God?

Nygren finds such questions to contain ideas which must be sorted and distinguished from basic Christian motifs. The idea of vicarious sacrifice is clearly central to the Christian view of atonement, but to conclude that the sacrifice is offered to God, and that it is presented from man's side and on man's behalf, is clearly not in line with essential and characteristic Christian motifs.

From one perspective it may seem altogether natural—even ethical—to think that man must make amends or offer reparation and satisfaction to God. But from the Christian point of view such thoughts are completely misleading. To claim that God must have satisfaction before releasing his grace is to misrepresent the nature of God's agape; and to think that man must meet his obligations and make reparation to God before he can accept God's grace and enter into fellowship with him is to refuse God's terms for fellowship and follow one's own. Fellowship with God is not on the basis of a *quid pro quo.* To interpret the atonement as though it were the payment of all man's debts to God easily comes to mean that God has received his due and that man now has a perfect right to expect that he will be admitted into fellowship with God. Such is the caricature of the Christian understanding of the God-relationship that results from the egocentric compromises that have found rootage in Christian theology.

HOLINESS OR SIN?

To express the contrast between Christian and non-Christian concepts of atonement, Nygren proposes a startling paradox: "Fellowship with God on the basis of holiness—that has been the age-long dream of humanity; fellowship with God on the basis of sin—that is the new message of Christianity, for it is exactly what 'the word of reconciliation' implies." [13] To say it in less paradoxical terms, in the Christian context atonement does not mean that we, from our side, of ourselves, or by way of a representative, raise ourselves to the level of holiness where we can rightfully commune with God; rather, atonement means that God lowers himself to our level and associates with us in the context of our sin. This is the radical new truth of Christianity. Nygren develops it to its fullest consequence when he sets forth the following propositions:

> (1) It is not holiness that leads to fellowship with God, but fellowship with God that leads to holiness; and (2) fellowship with God has not man's holiness as its aim, but is an end in itself.[14]

In arguing these points, Nygren refers to the contrast between a "natural and self-evident understanding of the God-relationship" and "the radical and extra-ordinary message of the gospel." Nygren sees this represented most clearly in the contrast between Roman Catholic and evangelical protestant interpretations of the God-relationship. Generally, Roman Catholic theology is seen to interpret man's fellowship with God as having its basis in works, whereas evangelical Christianity is seen to interpret fellowship with God as based on grace. This, says Nygren, is not altogether correct; the Roman Catholic also knows that salvation is by grace. The real difference is that in Roman Catholic theology fellowship with God is qualified with reference to holiness, while in evangelical Christianity fellowship with God is unqualified as far as man is concerned—i.e., it is realized in spite of sin. Roman Catholicism is therefore seen to represent the "natural" view of the God-relationship, while the essentially Christian view is found represented primarily in the churches of the Reformation.

The contrast between Roman Catholicism and evangelical Christianity appears nowhere more pronounced than in their doctrines of justification. The dispute on this point is no mere peripheral disagreement; it concerns the very structure of the God-relationship itself. Says Nygren, "When it comes to showing on what terms man is received into fellowship with God, the ways of Catholic and Evangelical Christianity part." [15] The Catholic way is expressed in the formula "faith formed by love" (*fides caritate formata*); the evangelical Christian way is proclaimed in the watchword "faith alone" (*sola fides*).

In analyzing this contrast, Nygren finds that what makes love such a central concern in Roman Catholic theology is that it serves as the fulfillment of the law. If love is found in man, then the essence of righteousness has been fulfilled—man is no longer a sinner, but holy, and God can assume him into fellowship. Fellowship with God is thus established, first by the sanctification of man (the infusion of love, i.e., holiness), then by the justification of man (assumption into divine fellowship). Fellowship with God is based on holiness. It was against this conception of justification that Luther launched his protest. For him, says Nygren, God's love is a "will to fellowship" which does not allow the presence of sin to set limits to love, but which stoops down to us in utter self-sacrifice and wills to have dealings with us in spite of our sin.[16] Such is the nature of God's grace. It is this loving will of God—the will to fellowship with sinners—to which faith holds fast, not to our own love, not to our own righteousness. Justification is God's declaration that sinners are acceptable in relation to him. We, on our side, are always sinners, nothing but sinners. But because of God's grace we are—paradoxically—"both righteous and sinners" (*simul iustus et peccator*). Fellowship with God is "by faith alone."

The reason fellowship with God can exist even on the basis of sin is that God is love and God's love is spontaneous and unmotivated. Nygren emphasizes this point to the extent that he opposes all attempts to justify justification and make it reasonable, either by reference to preconditions in man or by reference to subsequent results. Hence his second proposition—"Fellowship with God has not man's holiness as its aim, but is an end in itself." To seek to justify God's fellowship with sinners by reference to their ultimate sanctification is in reality to propose that God's love is a "seeking love"; and to seek to justify the sinner's faith in God by reference to some desirable outcome is to transform fellowship with God into an egocentric tool. Says Nygren, "To find a motivation for fellowship with God in something else [than fellowship with God] is the same as a denial of fellowship with God . . . a denial of divine love in the Christian sense, a denial of God's *agape*." [17] It is to say that what God loves is not the sinner but what can be made of the sinner, or that when God justifies the sinner it is not because he loves the sinner but because he anticipates fellowship with a future saint.

Such justifications of justification do of course have the effect of reducing the offensiveness of the idea that God loves sinners. But Nygren considers the advantage obtained at too great a loss. What is lost is the most characteristic element of Christianity: God's agape as spontaneous and unmotivated love. It is true that when Jesus addressed himself to sinners, the call to fellowship was usually accompanied with a call to repentance and conversion. But this does not mean that fellowship is conditioned on these other factors, or that love is a means and conversion the end. Love cannot be reduced to a means for some other end. If it is not an end in itself, love ceases to be love.[18]

AGAPE AND ATONEMENT

At this point Nygren suggests that the relationship between the Christian view of atonement and the Christian understanding of agape is not only very close; the two are simply different ways of saying the same thing. God's love and Christ's atonement "are not two separate things, but essentially one and the same."

> To speak of God's love and leave atonement out of account is to rob love of its divine depth. On the other hand, to speak of atonement and not to mean by it exclusively a work of divine love, is no longer to speak of atonement in the Christian sense of the word.[19]

But if God's agape and Christ's atonement are essentially the same thing, why continue to talk about atonement? Why not talk simply of God's love and forgiveness? Is not the nature of the divine agape so radical as to abolish the need for any work of atonement? If God is agape, why continue to speak as though atonement is necessary—as if love could not give itself directly without the intermediary influence of an atonement? Nygren raises these questions, but he considers the viewpoint fundamentally wrong. As he sees it, God's love, far from making atonement superfluous, is precisely the thing that makes atonement necessary.

One way to argue for the necessity of the atonement is to say that God's nature is not only love but also holiness; God's holiness requires atonement and God's love provides it. In the work of atonement, it is said, God's love has found a way to forgive which his holiness can accept. Although Nygren can appreciate this view as representing a serious attempt to come to terms with the mystery of the atonement, he still considers it misleading. For one thing, God's holiness and love are here split apart. Second, God's love is here considered "softer" in relation to sin than is God's holiness. And third, God's holiness is seen as powerless until it is somehow triggered by love. This, says Nygren, signals both a defective idea of love and an inferior concept of holiness.

In contrast, Nygren's own view is that if atonement is to be considered necessary, it must be with reference to a necessity which belongs to the essence of love itself. Nygren is quite emphatic on this point: "Atonement is necessary, not because God's love is holy, but because it is love." It is imperative that this be understood correctly, for without it "we shall never be able to understand how the atoning work of Christ, so far from implying any limitation of God's love, actually gives it its Christian depth." [20]

What is wrong with the view that love makes atonement superfluous is that both the nature of love and the seriousness of sin are understood superficially. The irreconcilable contradiction between God's love and human sin is blurred. Love is conceived as sentimentality, and sin is taken to be a moral defect. As Nygren sees it, to imagine that God's love should come to terms with sin any easier than does God's holiness is simply to show that one does not know either what God's love is or what human sin is. Sin, says Nygren, is much more serious than moral defects; it is a fundamental rebellion against God. It means that man has turned away from God, rejected God's sovereignty, and usurped God's place for himself. Sin is in its essence selfishness, not moral misdemeanors. And God's love is not sentimentality; rather, it is God's active will to rule the world with goodness. Love cannot easily forgive the self-assertion, egotism and self-centeredness which characterizes man's life. "Forgiveness can only exist in inseparable connection with real atonement." [21]

But what is atonement, then, and what is forgiveness?

Love, says Nygren, is God's will to fellowship. God cannot will fellowship and overlook man's rebellion. But neither can God will fellowship and wait for man to renounce his selfishness and return to his love. God's love cannot be a passive, waiting love; the power of selfishness is not broken that easily. "Love must take upon itself the burden which selfishness has caused but refuses to bear." [22] It must become what Luther calls "lost love."

This, to Nygren, is the deepest mystery of the atonement and the essence of forgiveness. God's love and man's selfishness—these are the two great opposites. To bring them together, something must be sacrificed. Selfishness sacrifices nothing, least of all itself. This is the meaning of "vicarious sacrifice": when selfish man refuses to conform to the divine will for fellowship, God's love submits itself to the conditions of human rebelliousness, not allowing human selfishness to set the limits of love. Agape gives itself away in the context of selfishness. It suffers itself to become lost love—spurned and trampled underfoot. As Paul expresses it, "For our sake he made him to be sin who knew no sin, so that in him we might become the righteousness of God" (2 Cor. 5:21).

Nygren has gone far, but he takes one step further, exploring the infinite depths of God's sacrificial love. We must speak with reserve, he says, about the possible fruits of a love that gives itself so recklessly, and not too easily subscribe to "the doctrine of the omnipotence of suffering love." [23] Any such emphasis on the ultimate pragmatism of love only obscures the fact that love takes a risk, that suffering is not a sure way to success, and that sacrifice is truly a sacrifice. The love which is set before us in the image of Christ is quite clearly *lost love*. Here we have the ultimate sacrifice, the most profound suffering of all, that love becomes lost. Not that love comes to an end—God does not stop loving because his love is rejected and trampled upon. Divine love remains, even when it is cast away. It is only in this way that love gains its victory—that it does not cease when it is lost. It is only in this sense that the cross of Christ becomes the sign of God's victory over all his enemies: God's love is crucified into triumph.

As a summation of Nygren's view of the atonement, let us use his own words:

> This, then, is what atonement in the Christian and Evangelical sense means: it means that God in his grace or unmotivated love stoops down to sinful man and seeks fellowship with him. Man the sinner breaks fellowship with God. God the Holy One restores fellowship with lost man; and he restores it, not when a man has first worked his way up to the level of God's holiness, but precisely at the point where it was broken, in the midst of man's sin.[24]

The cross is indeed the key symbol of Christianity!

Part Five

MAKER OF THE MODERN THEOLOGICAL MIND

XII. Nygren's Theological Character

Anders Nygren's is a complex personality—not that he is difficult to unscramble or hard to understand, but complex in the sense that he holds together within a single system of thought a number of elements of content and methodology that are usually separated and pursued in isolation from one another. Not that he is intellectually schizophrenic or paradoxical or inconsistent. In Nygren's mind there is no inconsistency in being involved in philosophy *and* in theology, in systematic theology *and* in biblical theology, in scientific theology *and* in Christian proclamation, in scholarly work *and* in active church ministry, in confessional explication *and* in ecumenical conversation. On the contrary, it is only when these and other relevant aspects of universality and particularity are included in the theologian's perspective and interest sphere that he has the basic qualifications for developing a theology that is doctrinally responsible, historically sound, intellectually mature, culturally relevant, and scientifically respectable. Nygren's own theological character is shaped in the interplay of all these elements of thought and inquiry. It is this fact that makes him such an excellent model for modern theologians and qualifies him uniquely for the distinction of being designated a "maker of the modern theological mind."

In trying to assess the theological character of Anders Nygren, one must be careful to observe how the many different emphases in his system of thought fit together. Evaluations based on partial inquiries and individual fragments are not likely to be very accurate. Moreover, since there is such a wide spectrum to Nygren's perspectives, the usual categories for classifying or placing scholars—liberal versus conservative, modernist versus fundamentalist—cannot be applied. If anything, Nygren must be described by way of a number of contrasting classifications—radical, fundamental, scientific, conservative. But even then the classifications cannot be used in the usual sense. Nygren is definitely a modern thinker, but he is not a modernist. He is concerned with fundamentals, but he is not a fundamentalist. He is clearly a liberal theologian, but he does not espouse theological liberalism. He is a critical thinker, but he does not subscribe to the doctrines of criticism. Anders Nygren's thought is both radical and conservative, both scientific and fundamental, but because it is all these things, at one and the same time, it is none of these things in the usual sense of the terms.

Nygren's critics have not always observed the complex combinations of factors contributing to the make-up of his thought. He has often fallen victim to critics and opponents whose perspectives are rather more narrowly delimited than his own and who consequently have little comprehension of the whole—and therefore little understanding of the details—of Nygren's thought-world. Some of Nygren's critics have had difficulties accepting his broad interests and involvements in questions of philosophy and scientific methodology; others have had problems understanding his definite concerns for the categorical separateness and autonomous meaning of religious experience and religious language. In the first context, Nygren has been criticized by conservative theologians for being engaged in extratheological inquiries and using natural perspectives and principles of thought, and by radical-minded positivists among the philosophers for attempting to place moral and religious inquiries within a framework which is supposed to be value-free and objective. In the second context, Nygren has been judged harshly both by idealistically oriented philosophers who would like to see a smooth correlation of religious and secular perspectives, and by aggressively apologetic theologians who would want the confrontation between faith and reason to be sharp and hard. Before attempting some clarification of the complexities of Nygren's theological character, we shall refer to a couple of Nygren's most vociferous opponents as examples of critics who have shown little regard for the broader scope and the minute refinements of Nygren's thought.[1]

TWO CRITICS

The first and perhaps most devastating criticism of Nygren's perspectives was issued in the 1950s by Gustaf Wingren, Nygren's successor in the chair of systematic theology at Lund University.[2] Issued first in the form of a series of articles in *Svensk teologisk kvartalskrift,* then in a public debate between the two men before the student body at the university, and finally in a book entitled *Theology in Conflict* in which Wingren squares off not only with Nygren, but also with Barth and Bultmann, Wingren's attacks were based on a point of view entirely unsympathetic with both the philosophical (scientific) and the theological (evangelical) emphases in Nygren's thought. Wingren has since continued his criticism in the 1970s, seeking to counteract the resurgence of interest in the so-called Lundensian methodology by minimizing the significance of the Nygren-Bring tradition in the life of the Lund faculty and declaring that as far as the students at Lund were concerned, with the late 1930s and early 40s, it was all over for the "Lundensians" at Lund.[3]

Wingren's own theological concern focuses on the "correct" interpretation of Scripture, on the one hand, and on the "right" presentation of the biblical message in the contemporary situation, on the other. The first requires a methodology that allows the Christian message not only to be studied by historical-systematic motif research but also to be proclaimed as the truth of God in the here and now. In both of these contexts, Wingren finds that Nygren's methodology fails. As he sees it, Nygren's philosophical orientation hinders the proper understanding of the biblical message.[4] Moreover, the concern for the truth and relevance of the gospel in the context of present existence is altogether "foreign" to Nygren's way of thinking.[5] Wingren finds it necessary, therefore, not simply to criticize certain features in Nygren's methodology, but to undertake what he calls "a purposive demolition of the religious-philosophical foundation" of Nygren's entire system.[6]

Wingren's heavy hand falls first on Nygren's critical philosophy of religion.[7] It has no reference to objective, transcendent realities but remains consistently within the subjective, anthropological realm. The validity of faith is demonstrated, not by reference to its truth value, but simply by reference to universal human values. Nygren's philosophy of religion, in fact, never gets beyond the limitations of human consciousness and cultural life. All of human culture is found to show some concern for the eternally valid, and it is this human concern for eternal validity which becomes Nygren's fundamental category of religion. But this sort of validity, in Wingren's perspective, is meaningless. It does not refer to anything positive. Nygren keeps his religious category altogether empty and devoid of content. It functions only as a question, and because the question is open, all sorts of answers are allowed to flow into it, all of them equally valid—and Christianity simply one among them. There is no objective way to determine what is valid and what is not; there is only a personal, subjective choice. But all choices are equally valid, and thus there is no validity except the choice itself. Validity, then, is no longer a question of truth. In Wingren's words, "any concern about the question of truth in theology is very quickly and radically eliminated from Nygren's view."[8]

Wingren next criticizes Nygren's scientific approach to systematic theology. One problem here is that Nygren isolates theology from theoretical criticism. He relies on the naïve assumption that faith does not need to defend itself against any attacks from without. Theology is given merely a descriptive, characterizing task; it becomes motif research, nothing more. The major problem, however, is that Nygren's scientific approach is not as open and scientific as he claims it to be. It is built on particular philosophical presuppositions. The questions that are asked are not at all the questions that Scripture or faith relate to, but are rather the questions posed by philosophy. Nygren, therefore, confronts the Christian message with the wrong questions—questions that are foreign to the biblical writings themselves. He divorces the Christian message from the basic question to which it is the answer, namely, "the pregnant question of guilt." He limits the Christian ethos within the realm of the agape-relationship and ignores the wider application of the law—that message which produces the sense of guilt, personal and social, to which the gospel is related.[9] These are fundamental flaws, says Wingren. For

> if it becomes apparent that the content of Scripture cannot be presented while those questions are ignored [namely, the questions of law and guilt] then it means that the method of approach in Nygren's theology clashes with the content of Scripture . . . the purely formal character of the question directed to the New Testament prevents a correct conception of the New Testament text.[10]

This, in Wingren's view, is precisely how seriously Nygren's method fails. It excludes in principle the kinds of analysis which are essential to the understanding of the biblical sources;[11] it is not, therefore, really a scientific method at all.[12]

Enough has been said to indicate the main thrust of Wingren's criticism. We shall leave aside the temptation to counter it on Nygren's behalf. That it is formulated on the basis of explicitly antiphilosophical and antievangelical standpoints is clear. Wingren is simply not interested in the attempt to lay any scientific foundations for theology by way of philosophy, and he is not at all concerned to perpetuate what he calls a pietistic type inquiry into the essentials of evangelical Christian faith and life.[13] The foundations of theology are not to be found in philosophy, but in Scripture. The Christian message is not merely a gospel of God's agape, but also a proclamation of the law of God. And Christian ethics is not only built on the assumptions of redemption and its consequences for Christian life, but also on the assumptions of creation and its implications for natural life. From Wingren's perspective, therefore, Nygren's theology is all wrong, and the reason is simply that the method is wrong.[14]

The second of Nygren's opponents to be looked at briefly here is Ingemar Hedenius, a popular cultural figure in Sweden during the second third of the twentieth century, and a philosopher of a radical positivistic stripe. Hedenius is interesting in our context because, although he represents a purely intellectual point of view, he questions Nygren not only on the philosophical adequacy of his perspectives but also on the theological adequacy of his methodology. Hedenius's attack, launched first in 1949 in a sharply pointed book entitled *Tro och vetande* (Faith and Knowing), and continued later in a debate before the student body at Lund University,[15] gained wide attention and caused Lundensian theology to lose much of its impact among the intellectuals to whom it had sought to direct itself.

Hedenius's argument rests on three particular postulates which he presupposes from the outset: (1) that religion is not merely piety but also the assertion of the truth-value of certain religious conceptions and convictions ("the religious-psychological postulate"); (2) that religious language is capable of being understood by believers and unbelievers alike ("the language-theoretical postulate"); and (3) that two truths cannot contradict each other ("the logical postulate").[16] Armed with these three scalpels, Hedenius proceeds to cut into the literary bodies of theologians, dead and living, both those who had attempted to *harmonize* faith and reason, those who had asserted that the two are entirely *dichotomous*, and those who had sought to sort out the relationship between them in terms of *two independent, autonomous, and equally valid forms of thought*—the latter, of course, being the Lundensian alternative. From Hedenius's perspective, and on the basis of his postulates, the Lundensian alternative is particularly weak. Not only does it represent a "hard-boiled denial of the truth-value of Christian faith"; it is full of "confused ideas," "empty speculation," "logical errors," "apologetic tricks," and "intellectual swindles."

Hedenius's interest focuses primarily on Nygren's theory of the autonomous contexts of meaning, and particularly the distinction which Nygren draws between the theoretical and the atheoretical contexts.[17] What makes this distinction interesting to Hedenius is Nygren's view that these contexts answer to altogether different questions. Only the theoretical context answers the question of truth; the atheoretical contexts—and the religious context among them—do not. The irritating aspect of the theory, to Hedenius, is that Nygren goes directly against two of his postulates. Not only is the religious-psychological postulate threatened; if Nygren is allowed to get away with his distinction of contexts or categories, the consequence is that the logical postulate cannot be strictly applied to statements of faith—which is precisely the way Hedenius desires to proceed in proving faith to be nonsensical. So Nygren must not be allowed to make this distinction. Hedenius ridicules, in fact, the suggestion that religious utterances do not answer the question of truth but express an entirely different dimension of meaning, namely, "the total relationship to God." "Truth," after all, means simply "holding something for true," "asserting that something is the case." So, according to Hedenius, to tear religious experience or religious statements out of relationship to that which is the case or that which is held to be true is to make a sham, an unreality, of religion itself. "Nygren must hold God's existence to be true if his theology is to hang together."[18] For what is a relationship to God without the assertion that God exists?

Hedenius next takes up Nygren's emphases that different ethical and religious points of view represent different motif contexts; that each of these contexts is organized around a single *grundmotiv,* an idea that forms the central principle within a given system of faith; and that these motif contexts cannot be proven true or false, but must be studied, on their own and in comparison with other such motif contexts, by way of scientific motif research. Hedenius does not understand how Nygren can speak of an "organic interconnection" between Christian ideas —between central and peripheral affirmations of faith—without seeing that this requires that the central motifs must be held as true. If they are not, the function of the central motifs as organizing principles within systems of faith would be logically impossible. Moreover, the comparison of different religions or faith systems would be meaningless. For if the Christian *agape*-motif is not held to be the true structure of God's relationship to the world, what possible sense is there in setting it up as the distinguishing mark of Christianity—that which is the center and core of all Christian faith and which sets it apart from all other faiths? The contrast between agape and eros is, after all, clearly

> a contradiction between two conceptions, one of which cannot be true if the other is, or vice versa; and the existence of the contradiction depends on the fact that they both make claim to being true while at the same time being logically incompatible.[19]

The upshot of Hedenius's argument is that the Lundensian theologians cannot be allowed to separate the atheoretical contexts of meaning from the theoretical. Religion without theoretical truth-claims is both impossible and improbable. Symbolic meaning without reference-value represents both an impoverished and overcomplicated use of language. Without the traditional truth-claims and reference-values, Christian theology would be a parody of what Christian faith is commonly understood to be—and, incidentally, only a shadow of what people like him, Hedenius, usually finds available to oppose. How bizarre Hedenius's criticism of Nygren can get is well exemplified in his—the avowed atheist's—final blast against the Lundensians:

> Atheists, dressed up as bishops and priests, who enjoy Christianity in another way than is normal. . . . A theology that is sliding, a systematic embarrassment on behalf of the gospel. . . .[20]

NYGREN'S THEOLOGICAL PROFILE

In evaluating any system of thought, one is clearly not able to do justice to the truth unless one is involved in the same sort of problematics which the system is designed to resolve, capable of applying truly critical perspectives to the analysis of various contexts and dimensions of thought, and willing to lay aside one's own preconceptions—one's own system of absolutes—and eager to learn how someone else's system works. Only one who is willing to listen will ultimately have the right to judge. Those who are not would be wiser to let other systems of thought alone altogether.

We have already pointed to the remarkable many-sideness of Nygren's philosophical and theological thought. That Nygren's critics have not always seen this—or seeing it, have not always understood it—is obvious from our references to Wingren and Hedenius. The usefulness of such criticism is clearly rather limited.

However, even those who are willing to listen, and who look at Nygren's thought system from within, are at times puzzled by what appears to be diametrically opposite tendencies in his thought. How, we ask, can he be so liberal and yet so fundamental, so tradition-oriented and yet so modern, so ecumenical and yet so dogmatic, so authoritative and yet so tentative? Or, more specifically, how can he be at one and the same time so radical in methodology and so conservative in content, so committed to fundamental Christian doctrine and so taken with scientific respectability, so open-ended in regard to modern thoughtforms and so definitive in regard to the Christian *grundmotiv*, so determined to identify the permanent and unchanging element in Christianity and so willing to accept the dynamics of history and historical relativity?

The answers to these questions must, of course, be derived from the analysis of Nygren's own thought. In one sense this entire book is an attempt to answer such and similar questions. But if we should try once more, here at the end, to make clear how Nygren's theological character is made up, and how he is able to hold together so many different interests and emphases, the most useful procedure may well be to explain in what sense he is radical, in what sense he is scientific, in what sense he is conservative, and in what sense he is fundamental.

Nygren's Radicality

From one point of view it is clear that Nygren's methodology represents a radical departure from certain approaches and perspectives that have been so common among Christian theologians as to become virtually synonymous with theology. To start the development of the theological perspective, not with the intratheological assumptions of revelation, Scripture, tradition, or faith, but with an analysis of human experience and the transcendental deduction of the elemental categories of human awareness and meaning—i.e., with the philosophical analysis of basic epistemological issues—is certainly different from the traditional theological stance, *fides quaerens intellectum*. It represents an anthropocentrism which is more in line with the perspectives of the opponents of faith than with anything Christian theologians have tended to do and say in the past. And to accept, as Nygren does, the limits of reason as being imposed even on faith, and thus to forswear all claims to superior knowledge or special metaphysical insight, is obviously not usual when it comes from a member of the theological community or a bishop of the church. It is the expression of an empiricism which is more typical of a scientist than of a theologian. Yet this is precisely what Nygren does, and so he is considered radical.

It is important to understand, however, that although from one point of view Nygren's methodology represents a radical departure from accepted patterns of theological thought, from another perspective it is nothing more than an attempt to realign the disciplines of philosophy of religion and theology with all other forms of human thought or knowledge, and thus to establish some semblance of harmony—or at least mutual recognition and respect—between the various branches of science. From this point of view, Nygren's radicality is simply his willingness to take up for discussion the methodological questions that lie at the roots of all science, theology included. That he is able to do so, and that he is willing to draw the consequences of such inquiries in the definition and delimitation of his own philosophical and theological concerns, is not something that ought to be rejected simply because it is different and unusual. On the contrary, it ought to be taken as a serious challenge to becoming involved in the basic issues, as they are perceived, and in the quest for answers, wherever they may be found.

With this understanding of Nygren's methodology, one discovers that Nygren is not in fact so radical a theologian, after all. He does not, for example, propose to discard the claim that the disciplines of philosophy of religion and theology have unique functions and possess their own kind of meaning. Neither does he suggest that these disciplines, whose scientific status is difficult to defend, should be replaced by some other, more easily defensible disciplines. Nygren's radicality never develops into reductionism. He is committed to the viability of his disciplines, their religious as well as scientific character, and he engages himself actively in defending them against any intrusions by other members of the scientific community as well as any obfuscations on the part of the religious community. Nygren, in short, is a well-balanced radical.

Nygren's Scientism

Nygren at times comes across to his readers as a rather naïve believer in the virtues of science. There is evidence in Nygren's thought to support such a judgment. He seems willing to accept without demur the dominance of the scientific worldview over the mind set of modern man. He abhors metaphysics as representing unverifiable speculation. He has an aversion to subjectivism and all other evidence of methodological arbitrariness. Nygren does not think that philosophy, philosophy of religion, or theology will have a beggar's chance of respectable existence in the modern age without establishing their scientific respectability in the way all other scientific disciplines do—by reference to a knowable object of study, in terms of a viable scientific interest, and by way of an objective scientific method. And he does not think the human mind can ever claim to have laid hold of ultimate or absolute truths; only tentative, hypothetical conceptions of truth, truths that are open to verification and falsification by reference to historical-empirical facts, are within the grasp of science. Nygren is even willing to consider the concept "truth" a uniquely scientific or theoretical concept, and not to make truth-claims on behalf of atheoretical contexts or categories of meaning that are marked by subjective or commitmental standpoints at all. There is thus a distinctly positivistic tendency in Nygren's view of science—even the sciences of religion or theology.

In saying this, however, one must also observe that Nygren's conception of science is double-edged. It cuts inward, to the core of the scientific consciousness, to the questions concerning the nature and extent of human knowledge (science); and it cuts outward, to the practical application of scientific principles in the confrontation of man with the given facts of his existence (the sciences). Nygren's scientism is not a superficial attempt to latch on to popular scientific thought and thus to gain a modicum of acceptance for the theological message. Neither does it represent an uncritical move to make philosophy of religion or theology captive to the processes or procedures that have proved so useful in other sciences. Nygren is deeply involved in the philosophical inquiry into the nature of science—and he must be. As a philosopher of religion and a theologian, he cannot afford to be absent when the analysis of the nature of human knowledge is taking place. Philosophy and theology are, after all, forms of human knowledge. Nygren is also deeply concerned to develop scientific procedures that are uniquely suited to the tasks that philosophers of religion and theologians perform. As he sees it, the principles of science are the same in all the sciences, but scientific procedures must be rethought and reformulated within each individual scientific discipline.

It is clear, therefore, that when one considers the deeper dimensions of Nygren's scientism, he cannot be described as a victim of the infantile maladies of positivistic naïveté and rationalistic enthusiasm. Nygren's is a critical mind set. His commitment to science is a commitment to knowledge and sense, to meaning and truth—all types of knowledge, every kind of sense, each dimension of meaning, and any form of truth. He is not a blind believer, affirming science's every move and result. Only when science is so oriented as to provide objective insight and inclusive understanding of the realities and validities of human existence in the world is science on the right track. It is only with reference to a science so oriented that Nygren is concerned to claim the distinction of being a scientist. Simply put, Nygren's is not a naïve belief in science at all.

Nygren's Conservatism

It could well be argued, as indeed it has, that when Nygren seeks to guard the autonomy of philosophy of religion and theology and for this reason isolates religious meaning within a separate and unique category of experience, he is entering the arena of methodological studies not for purposes of opening avenues of dialogue and interaction between religious awareness and all other forms of knowledge, but rather to draw lines and build fences behind which these disciplines can exist and function in complete independence of the other sciences and without the threat of criticism or challenge from without. Nygren's statement, "Let religion be religious," sounds like a very conservative motto. His emphasis that religious statements can only be understood on the basis of their own particular presuppositions seems like a revival of theological exclusivism, and his restriction of faith reflection within the religious context of meaning, without a legitimate concern to challenge the autonomy of other categories of thought, appears like a new edition of world-estranged pietism. Nygren is easily conceived as an apologetic theologian of a distinctly conservative stripe.

One should note, however, that although Nygren's standpoint bears certain resemblances of a conservative mind set, his conservatism is clearly of an enlightened sort. It is as a result of extensive philosophical analyses of the phenomena of human experience as well as detailed logical investigations of the presuppositions of meaning within various categories of thought and language that Nygren comes to the conviction that religious awareness is categorically different from theoretical knowledge, aesthetic sense, and moral consciousness. Moreover, when he distinguishes the religious context of meaning from science, art, and morality, Nygren is not for a moment suggesting that the religious consciousness is sufficient unto itself or that it can presume to take over the functions of the other categories of awareness. Nygren's conservatism does not have the character of religious isolationism; neither is it marked by religious imperialism. It is simply the result of Nygren's desire to avoid logical confusion in the relationship between the different dimensions of human experience, and of his commitment to interpret the various categories of meaning and language—all of them—on the basis of their own particular presuppositions.

If one understands the background for Nygren's claim that religious awareness represents an autonomous context of meaning, one will recognize that Nygren's views are not so conservative after all. Nygren does not, for example, allow the religious context of meaning to be based on presuppositions that are beyond analysis. Neither does he permit religious language to operate without respect for rules of logical consistency and common sense. His conservatism does not become a cover for irrationalism and paradoxicality. He is clearly committed to the logical explication of the meaning of the faith, and he pursues this meaning—and proclaims it—in the broad daylight of intellectual honesty. Nygren's, in other words, is a rather extraordinary kind of conservatism.

Nygren's Fundamentalism

The observation, often made, that Nygren's theology represents a new form of evangelical orthodoxy or fundamentalism can easily be supported by reference to several facets of Nygren's thought. For one thing, he is definitely concerned to identify the central and essential motifs of Christian faith. For another, he is clearly determined to root out any and all conceptions of Christianity that are in any way contradictory of what he considers to be the true, evangelical meaning of the gospel. His commitment to Scripture as the source of first priority is clear. His relationship to theological traditions is a critical one, and his criterion of evaluation is an explicitly evangelical, New Testament-oriented conception of Christianity. His interpretation of the Christian faith and God-relationship in consistently theocentric terms in reminiscent of neoorthodoxy.

However, to note these signs of orthodoxy or fundamentalism, and not at the same time acknowledge some of the refinements that are part of Nygren's evangelical perspective, is to misunderstand the nature of Nygren's orientation and misrepresent his theology altogether. Nygren's concern for the fundamentals of the faith is the motivation for historical-critical systematic inquiry, not the expression of absolutist-authoritarian dogmatism. His relationship to Scripture is formed by historical-critical biblical scholarship, not by fundamentalistic brands of biblicism or literalism. And Nygren's studies of theological traditions are informed by the awareness of historical relativity and cultural conditioning. Clearly, then, Nygren's fundamentalism has nothing to do with fundamentalistic perspectives or fundamentalistic methodologies. His, rather, is a fundamentalism that is schooled in the methodology of science and held in check by the requirements of responsible scholarship.

When Nygren's fundamentalism is set in context within the larger methodological structure that Nygren has built, it turns out to be a fundamentalism of a peculiar sort—and really not, in a technical sense, fundamentalism at all. Nygren does not, for example, predetermine what is to be considered normative truth concerning faith or doctrine. In his view, the essence of Christian faith and doctrine will come clear only as a result of historical-critical investigations into the many manifestations of Christian faith and life that have appeared throughout history. Again, Nygren does not predefine what form the presentation of the central motifs of Christian faith is to take in the present. As he sees it, doctrinal explication is an ongoing task; in each era, in each culture, theologians must do the work of theology anew—in the thought-forms of the time and place, and in full view of the circumstances of life within which men live. Nygren's, then, is a sensible form of fundamentalism.

We have looked at four contrasting characteristics of Nygren's thought, and we have sought to explain how with further inquiry and reflection the complexities of Nygren's theological stance can be seen to hold together. Similar explications could be made with reference to Nygren's historicism, objectivism, confessionalism, and relativism. Such elements are definitely present in his thought, but they interact and temper each other in such a way as to blend into an integral and consistent system of thought. Moreover, since they do interact and temper each other, the bearer of the thought-system cannot be tagged by reference to preconceived notions of what such characteristics usually mean. Anders Nygren's theological character is complex; he cannot quickly be classified, pigeon-holed, and stacked away. And he cannot easily be ignored. His thought has so deeply infiltrated the fabric of contemporary philosophical and theological thinking, at so many points and in so many ways, that we shall not soon be able to forget him.

Anders Nygren is a theologian in search of a proper philosophical base, an appropriate theological method, and a responsible understanding of Christian essence. Such are his contributions to the making of the modern theological mind.

NOTES AND BIBLIOGRAPHY

Notes

PART ONE

Chapter I

1. A fuller description of the roots of Nygren's thought is contained in my book, *A Framework for Faith: Lundensian Theological Methodology in the Thought of Ragnar Bring*, 1970, chapters 1 and 2. (Publication information on this and subsequent titles that is not given in the notes, may be found in the bibliography.)

2. This term is used here in the European fashion, broadly referring to the many disciplines of knowledge or "sciences," not in the more exclusive sense of the natural or social sciences.

3. Gustav Aulén's major work is *The Faith of the Christian Church*, first published in Sweden 1917, since then in six Swedish editions, two English translations, and in various other languages. The latest English edition was published in paperback by Fortress Press, 1973.

4. Arvid Runestam, *Svensk teologisk kvartalskrift* 2 (1926) : 93.

5. Arvid Runestam, "Gudstro och självkännedom," in *Ordet och tron*, 1931, pp. 138–39.

6. Cf. Nathan Söderblom, *Uppenbarelsereligion*, 1930.

7. See, for example, Einar Billing's *De etiska tankarna i urkristendomen*, 1907.

8. This commitment is explicitly set forth in the introduction to *The Faith of the Christian Church*.

9. So, for example, Nels Ferré, *Swedish Contributions to Modern Theology*, 2nd ed., 1967.

10. This has been more closely analyzed in my book, *A Framework for Faith*, pp. 21–26.

Chapter II

1. The following is based, primarily, on the biography of Anders Nygren in *Svenska män och kvinnor*, vol. 5, 1949, and on Nygren's "Intellectual Autobiography" in *The Philosophy and Theology of Anders Nygren*, ed., Charles W. Kegley, 1970, pp. 3–29.
2. The *teol. cand.* degree with *practicum* is the graduate-professional degree for ministers in the Church of Sweden.
3. Gustav Aulén, *Från mina 96 år*, 1975, p. 91.
4. Nygren, "Intellectual Autobiography," p. 29.
5. Ibid., p. 5. 6. Ibid., p. 6. 7. Ibid., p. 9.
8. Ibid., p. 16. 9. Ibid., p. 26. 10. Ibid., p. 27.
11. Ibid., p. 26. 12. Ibid., p. 27. 13. Ibid., p. 29.

PART TWO

Chapter III

1. Thor Hall, *A Framework for Faith*, p. 74.
2. The following analysis is based in the main on chapters III to VIII of *Meaning and Method*. In these chapters Nygren makes repeated references to his earlier works, and insofar as these are relevant to our purposes here they will be included in subsequent notes. The reader is encouraged to compare the present overview of Nygren's thought with my earlier analyses, "Lundensian Methodology as Formulated by Anders Nygren," in *A Framework for Faith*, pp. 51–70, and "Nygren's Ethics," in *The Philosophy and Theology of Anders Nygren*, ed., Kegley, pp. 263–81.
3. Nygren has developed this positive function of metaphysics further in an early essay, entitled "Den metafysiska filosofiens betydelse," *Bibelforskaren*, 1918. He refers also to works by J. Agassi and Karl Popper which focus on the stimulus that metaphysics can give to science.
4. Interestingly, Nygren indicates that he had developed this universal criterion of scientific procedure already in 1928. Cf. *Meaning and Method*, p. 67, n. 1.
5. Ibid., pp. 82–83. 6. Ibid., p. 97.
7. Nygren subscribes to Karl Popper's famous "theory of falsification" at this point. He says that it involves "a new start" in philosophy which has the potential of revolutionizing our understanding of empirical knowledge and the conditions under which it can be had. Ibid., p. 113.
8. Ibid., p. 120. 9. Ibid., p. 129.

10. Quoted by Nygren from H. Feigl, "Logical Empiricism," in *Readings in Philosophical Analysis,* ed. H. Feigl and W. Sellars, p. 15.

11. Nygren, *Meaning and Method,* p. 221. 12. Ibid., p. 223.

Chapter IV

1. The following is based in the main on chapters IX–XI of Nygren, *Meaning and Method.*

2. The title of one of Nygren's chapters is, "From Atomism to Contexts of Meaning." This was also the title of Nygren's contribution to the *Christian Century's* "How My Mind Has Changed" series; the article is in fact incorporated in the chapter.

3. Nygren refers to Frege's essay, "Über Sinn und Bedeutung," published 1892, as being a short but penetrating analysis of the two concepts.

4. Nygren is particularly referring to Ludwig Wittgenstein's *Philosophical Investigations,* published 1958.

5. Quoted from Ludwig Wittgenstein, *Blue Book,* 1958, p. 69.

6. Quoted from Bertrand Russell, *An Inquiry Into Meaning and Truth,* 1940, p. 34.

7. Quoted from Ludwig Wittgenstein, *Tractatus,* 1922, 3.3.

8. The question might well be asked why Nygren has left both of the major tasks of analytical philosophy unfulfilled—the presuppositional analysis and the systematic integration of presuppositional categories. I have suggested an answer in another context. Cf. *A Framework for Faith,* pp. 90–92, 223–35.

9. Cf. Anders Nygren, *Essence of Christianity,* 1960, pp. 24–37.

10. Nygren, *Meaning and Method,* p. 275.

11. Ibid., p. 278. 12. Ibid., p. 276.

13. Ibid., p. 296. Nygren is evidently here anxious to indicate the independent presuppositional character of the ultimate principle of unity among the presuppositions. This is important to observe. Nygren has had a tendency to regard the religious category of "eternity" both as the specific presupposition within the religious context of meaning and as the ultimate principle of unity among all presuppositions whatever. He even suggests this in *Meaning and Method,* p. 343. Nygren's more formal concept of the presupposition of presuppositions is perhaps most clearly set forth in *Filosofisk och kristen etik,* 1923, where he suggests that the ultimate, meta-presuppositional principle of presuppositional integration is the following: "If an individual judgment is valid, certain presuppositions must be valid also." The problem with such an open statement of principle is of course that it gives no shape or structure to the system of integration. Nygren seems caught on the horns of a dilemma.

14. Nygren, *Meaning and Method,* p. 300.

15. The phrase is taken from the title of my article in *Interpretation,* 1969, pp. 158 ff. Uncharacteristically for Nygren, it is taken entirely out of context!

16. Nygren is critical in this context both of the existentialist demythologization program of Bultmann, the humanistic secularization hermeneutic of Schubert Ogden and Paul M. van Buren, and the idealistic correlation method of Paul Tillich. For Nygren's extensive discussion of these hermeneutical approaches, cf. *Meaning and Method,* pp. 303–325.

17. Ibid., p. 330. 18. Ibid., p. 334.

19. Ibid., p. 337. 20. Ibid., p. 341.

21. Nygren refers in this context to his earlier considerations of the religious category, *Religiöst apriori,* 1921, *Det religionsfilosofiska grundproblemet,* 1921, *Det bestående i kirstendomen,* 1922, "Är evighetskategorien en religiös kategori?" 1922, and "Till frågan om den transcendentala metodens användbarhet inom religionsfilosofien," 1923.

22. Nygren, *Meaning and Method,* p. 344.

23. These are well-known specifications of the experience of religion which Nygren first developed in *Det bestående i kristendomen.* Cf. Nygren, *Essence of Christianity,* pp. 38–48.

24. Ibid., p. 28.

Chapter V

1. Cf. for example Anders Nygren, *Filosofi och motivforskning,* 1940, p. 31; *Meaning and Method,* pp. 343, 360 ff.

2. We shall return to Nygren's definition of the task of theology in chapter VII. For the analysis of the task of philosophy of religion, cf. chapter IV.

3. Sigfrid von Engeström, "Arvet från Albrecht Ritschl . . . ," in *Nordisk teologi. Ideer och män,* 1955, p. 195.

4. Cf. Nygren, *Essence of Christianity,* p. 38.

5. Cf. above, chapter IV, the sections entitled "The Religious Context of Meaning" and "The Category Problem."

6. Nygren *Religiöst apriori,* pp. 170–71. Cf. also *Det religionsfilosofiska grundproblemet,* chapter IV:9; *Essence of Christianity,* pp. 38–39.

7. The following is based on the section "Religion" in Nygren, *Det bestående i kristendomen.* Cf. *Essence of Christianity,* pp. 39–48.

8. Cf. Nygren's reference to Christianity as "a historical realization of the religious category," "the only realization that can come into consideration for us [Christians]." *Dogmatikens vetenskapliga grundläggning,* 1922, p. 54.

9. The clearest statement of this basic contrast is found in Anders

Nygren, "Egoism och religion," *Svensk teologisk kvartalsskrift* 3 (1927):129–50; also in *Urkristendom och reformation,* 1932. Cf. also *Agape and Eros,* vols. 1 and 2.

10. Cf. *Filosofisk och kristen etik,* 1923; also *Etiska grundfrågor,* 1926.

11. For a defense of the typological procedures that have characterized Lundensian motif research, see Benkt-Erik Benktson, *Adam—vem är du?* 1976.

12. Cf. Nygren's "Additional Note" on various contributions by other scholars toward the further development of motif research, in *Meaning and Method,* pp. 384 ff.

13. The Working Group on Scandinavian Theology of the American Academy of Religion held a session on this subject at the annual meeting in San Francisco, December 1977. I presented a keynote paper at the session which was subsequently published in *Religion in Life* 57, no 2 (Summer 1978), under the title "Anders Nygren's Approach to the Methodological Issues in Inter-Faith Dialogue." Grateful acknowledgment is made of a generous grant from the American Philosophical Society in support of this part of our Nygren project.

14. Nygren, *Det religionsfilosofiska grundproblemet,* p. 150.

15. I am aware of the parallels between this line of argument, developed on the basis of Nygren's perspectives, and that of H. Richard Niebuhr in *The Meaning of Revelation.* Nygren has himself not taken account of this work by Niebuhr.

16. Nygren quotes with approbation Friedrich Schleiermacher's famous definition of Christianity: "Christianity is essentially distinguished from other faiths by the fact that everything in it is related to the redemption accomplished by Jesus of Nazareth." From *The Christian Faith,* 1922, p. 9.

17. Nygren, *Meaning and Method,* pp. 296–97.

PART THREE

Chapter VI

1. In this chapter I rely on a variety of sources, but primarily Nygren's *Filosofi och motivforskning,* 1940, and *Meaning and Method,* 1972. Readers are encouraged to consult my study of Lundensian methodology, *A Framework for Faith,* 1970, and a number of essays in *The Philosophy and Theology of Anders Nygren,* ed., Charles W. Kegley, 1970, particularly those by Philip S. Watson, Bernhard Erling, and myself.

2. Although "dogmatic theology" is a general concept that may be applicable to any dogmatic context or to any religion, it has usually been taken as a technical term for Christian theology. We shall follow

this practice here. Nygren is himself a Christian theologian, and all that he says about theological methodology is related to the task of Christian dogmatics.

3. Cf. Nygren, *Filosofi och motivforskning*, pp. 75–76.

4. In another context, I have drawn the comparison with specific reference to their relations to Kant. Cf. *A Framework for Faith*, pp. 21–26.

5. Nygren's own statement of these requirements is most clearly set forth in *Filosofi och motivforskning*, particularly in the essays entitled "Hur är filosofi som vetenskap möjlig?" (How Is Philosophy as a Science Possible?), "Till frågan om teologiens objektivitet" (On the Question of the Objectivity of Theology), and "Systematisk teologi och motivforskning" (Systematic Theology and Motif Research).

6. Ibid., p. 168. 7. *Meaning and Method*, p. 371.

Chapter VII

1. Nygren, *Filosofi och motivforskning*, p. 180.

2. Nygren's essay on the subject is entitled "Till frågan on teologiens objektivitet." It was first published in 1922, then reprinted in *Filosofi och motivforskning*.

3. Cf. ibid., pp. 181 ff.

4. I have taken the liberty of updating these points in line with Nygren's more recent terminology and so as to be consistent with the language utilized above. For the original form of this material, cf. ibid., p. 183. Cf. also my book, *A Framework for Faith*, pp. 68–69.

5. Two major essays by Nygren explicate these matters, namely "Det självklaras roll i historien," English translation, "The Role of the Self-Evident in History," in *Journal of Religion* 28, no. 4 (1948); and "Atomism eller sammanhang i historiesynen," in *Filosofi och motivforskning*. The discussion here is based on Nygren's most recent analysis of these subjects, in *Meaning and Method*, pp. 352 ff.

6. Ibid., p. 353. 7. Ibid. 8. Ibid., p. 354.

9. Ibid., p. 355. 10. Ibid., p. 356.

11. Cf. above, chapter V, the section entitled "Religion and the Religions." The following paragraphs reflect viewpoints which Nygren has presented in *Meaning and Method*, pp. 360–61.

12. Ibid., p. 361. 13. Ibid.

14. Ibid., p. 371. 15. Ibid., p. 378.

Chapter VIII

1. The following discussion is primarily dependent on *Meaning and Method*, pp. 363–65.

2. Ibid., p. 364.

3. Nygren, *Filosofi och motivforskning*, pp. 46–47.

4. Cf. ibid., p. 78; *Agape and Eros,* 1953, p. 35. The following discussion is dependent for the most part on *Meaning and Method,* pp. 372–73.

5. Nygren, *Agape and Eros,* p. 35.

6. Cf. above, chapter V, the section entitled "Religion and the Religions," and Chapter VII, the section entitled "The Integrity of Faith."

7. Cf. the full quotation above, pp. 140–41.

8. Cf. above, chapter VII, the section entitled "The Integrity of Faith."

9. Nygren, *Meaning and Method,* p. 361.

10. Cf. Nygren *Agape and Eros,* pp. 35 ff; *Filosofi och motivforskning,* pp. 45–62; *Meaning and Method,* pp. 362–3, 376 ff. See also my book *A Framework for Faith,* pp. 64–66.

PART FOUR

Chapter IX

1. Nygren's *The Permanent Element in Christianity* and *The Atonement as a Work of God* are brought together in a single volume, published in English under the title *Essence of Christianity,* 1960.

2. The following discussion is based on Nygren, *Essence of Christianity,* pp. 11–24.

3. Cf. above, chapter VIII, the section entitled "A Historical Method."

4. Cf. above, chapter V, the section entitled "Christianity as Religious Type."

5. The following discussion is based on Nygren, *Essence of Christianity,* pp. 49–57.

6. Cf. above, chapter IV, the sections entitled "The Religious Context of Meaning" and "The Category Problem"; also chapter V, the section entitled "The Nature of Religion."

7. Quoted from Schleiermacher, *The Christian Faith,* p. 9.

8. Quoted from Gustav Aulén, *Våra tankar om Kristus,* 1921, p. 3.

9. Nygren, *Essence of Christianity,* p. 57.

10. Ibid., pp. 51–52. 11. Ibid., p. 54.

12. Cf. Nygren, *Essence of Christianity,* pp. 58–62.

13. Ibid., pp. 60–61. 14. Ibid., p. 62.

Chapter X

1. Translated from the Swedish edition of Nygren, *Den kristna kärlekstanken,* Vol. 1, 1930, p. 4.

2. Nygren argues in this context that Christianity not only represents an answer to the categorical question; it has a certain influence on the formulation of the questions as well. For example, in regard to

ethics, Christianity has taken the question of "the good" out of the individualistic perspective and into a communal perspective; in regard to the religious question, Christianity has transferred the consideration of "the eternal" from the egocentric orientation to the theocentric orientation. Whether this Christian "bending" of the categorical questions is consistent with Nygren's principal emphasis on the formality and openness of the presuppositional categories is doubtful. Nygren seems to have become aware of this problem himself; he has not to our knowledge made this point in any other context.

3. Nygren finds the radicality of *agape* well illustrated in parables of Jesus, especially in the parables of the prodigal son (Luke 15:11–32) and the workers in the vineyard (Matthew 20:1–16).

4. Nygren, *Den kristna kärlekstanken,* I:74.

5. Nygren supports this interpretation with the following quotation from Rudolf Bultmann: "It is therefore stupid to say—and this again is possible only in association with the humanistic ideal of man—that a justifiable self-love, a necessary standard of self-respect, must precede love of neighbor, since the command runs 'love your neighbor *as yourself.*' Self-love is thus presupposed. Yes, it is indeed presupposed, but not as something which man must learn, which must be expressly required of him. It is the attitude of the natural man which must be overcome." Quoted here from the English edition of *Jesus and the Word,* 1958, p. 116.

Chapter XI

1. Einar Billing, *Forsoningen,* 1908, Gustaf Aulén, *Den kristna försoningstanken,* 1930 (Engl. trans. *Christus Victor,* 1931); Ragnar Bring, "Der Mittler und das Gesetz," 1966; *Christus und das Gesetz,* 1969.

2. Nygren, *Essence of Christianity,* p. 81.

3. In the following discussion I am relying on Philip S. Watson's translation, "The Atonement as a Work of God," in Nygren, *Essence of Christianity,* pp. 81–128.

4. Ibid., p. 83. 5. Ibid., p. 85. 6. Ibid., p. 88.

7. Ibid., p. 89. 8. Ibid., p. 91. 9. Ibid., pp. 92–93.

10. Nygren refers to Isaiah 6:1–7 as "the finest documentation" of what theocentric religion is all about. Ibid., p. 94.

11. Ibid., p. 96. 12. Ibid., p. 97. 13. Ibid., p. 101.

14. Ibid., p. 102. 15. Ibid., p. 103.

16. Ibid., p. 104. 17. Ibid., pp. 110, 111.

18. To illustrate this, Nygren refers to the criticism often directed toward Christian charity, namely, that it is used for the purposes of propaganda and that it is not therefore a real and genuine love, only a tool that is used for ulterior purposes. Ibid., p. 112.

19. Ibid., p. 113. 20. Ibid., pp. 118, 119.
21. Ibid., pp. 121–22. 22. Ibid., p. 123.
23. Ibid., p. 125. 24. Ibid., pp. 107 f.

PART FIVE

Chapter XII

1. The fullest and most responsible critique of Nygren's thought is contained in Charles W. Kegley's volume, *The Philosophy and Theology of Anders Nygren.* Reviews of *Meaning and Method* are now appearing in major theological journals. To date, the most detailed and balanced review of this work is Van A. Harvey's, in *Religious Studies Review* 1 (Sept. 1975) : 13–19.

2. A fuller analysis of Wingren's criticism of Nygren is included in my book, *A Framework for Faith,* pp. 208–211.

3. Cf. Gustaf Wingren, "Was geschah eigentlich in Lund in den dreissiger Jahren?" *Theologische Literaturzeitung* 97 (1972) : 886–90. Wingren here rewrites the history of the 30s and 40s to show that as the Lundensian methodology, under Bring's influence, turned more and more away from philosophical and systematic concerns toward preoccupation with purely historical investigations—tradition research, Luther studies, source analysis—he and other students at Lund at the time turned against their major teachers and followed the lead of Herbert Ohlson, then a *docent* at Lund. Ohlson was "a true historian of doctrine," a Lundensian à la Bring, but a Luther scholar who through the study of the historical sources discovered the importance in Christian thought of the motifs of creation and commandments—motifs entirely ignored in Nygren's one-sided agape studies, and motifs which he, Wingren, subsequently made his own primary concerns. Says Wingren, "What we published after that was historical theology, and in that we were of course 'Lundensians'; but motif research it was not. It laid the basis, instead, for a critique of motif research."

4. Gustav Wingren *Theology in Conflict,* 1958, p. 17.

5. Ibid., p. 88. 6. Ibid., p. 90. 7. Ibid., pp. 3 ff.
8. Ibid., p. 9. 9. Ibid., pp. 16–17. 10. Ibid., pp. 18–19.
11. Ibid., p. 22. 12. Ibid., p. 90. 13. Ibid., pp. 78–79.

14. Ibid., p. 81. That Wingren has been influential in turning some of Nygren's readers from seriously grappling with his thought is evidenced in a recent review of Nygren's *Meaning and Method,* published in *Scottish Journal of Theology* 28 (1975), and written by W. A. Whitehouse. The reviewer confesses that he had "digested the book, with considerable benefit though with dispiriting results overall," when it occurred to him to refer to Wingren's earlier critique of Nygren. In the light of Wingren's *Theology in Conflict,* he found "the defects" of

Nygren's method "exposed" with "devastating precision." Says Whitehouse (p. 576), "A Christian cleric who is ready to sell out so completely to 'the modern conception of life' and the modern interpretation of 'scientific,' and to the philosophy in which these modernities are articulated, disqualifies himself, on the evidence, from achieving that conformity of Christian thought to its object which truly deserves to be called 'scientific.' "

15. Actually, the two men were supposed to share the platform, but Hedenius refused. He presented *his* side of the argument one week, and Nygren *his* two weeks later. Nygren chided Hedenius a little, suggesting that philosophers ever since Plato had done their best work in dialogue, not by way of monologue—comments which came back to haunt him some time later, when Wingren challenged him to public debate.

16. Ingemar Hedenius, *Tro och vetande,* 1949, pp. 64 ff.

17. Ibid., pp. 163 ff. 18. Ibid., p. 180.

19. Ibid., pp. 193–94. 20. Ibid., pp. 218–19.

Bibliography

Aulén, Gustaf. *Christus Victor*. London: SPCK, 1931.

———. *The Faith of the Christian Church*. Philadelphia: Muhlenberg Press, 1960.

———. *Från mina 96 år*. Stockholm: Verbum, 1975.

———. *Den kristna försoningstanken*. Stockholm: Diakonistyrelsen, 1930.

———. *Våra tankar om Kristus*. Stockholm: Sveriges kristliga studentrörelse, 1921.

Benktson, Benkt-Erik. *Adam—vem är du?* Lund: Håkan Ohlssons Förlag, 1976.

Billing, Einar. *De etiska tankarna i urkristendomen*. Ur kristendomens historia och tankevärld, vol. 3. Uppsala: Schultz, 1907.

———. *Försoningen*. Uppsala: Almquist och Wiksell, distr., 1908.

Bring, Ragnar. *Christus und das Gesetz*. Leiden: Brill, 1969.

———. "Der Mittler und das Gesetz," *Kerygma und Dogma*, vol. 12, 1966.

Bultmann, Rudolf. *Jesus and the Word*. New York: Scribners, 1958.

Engeström, Sigfrid von. "Arvet från Albrecht Ritschl i den svenska teologien." In *Nordisk teologi. Ideer och män*. Lund: Gleerup, 1955.

Feigl, H. "Logical Empiricism." In *Readings in Philosophical Analysis*. Edited by H. Feigl, and W. Sellars. New York: Prentice Hall, 1949.

Ferré, Nels F. S. *Swedish Contributions to Modern Theology*. 2nd ed. New York: Harper & Row, 1967.

Frege, Gottlob. "Über Sinn und Bedeutung." *Zeitschrift für Philosophie und philosophische Kritik,* New Series, vol. 100 (1892) : 25–50.

Hall, Thor. *A Framework for Faith: Lundensian Theological Methodology in the Thought of Ragnar Bring.* Leiden: Brill, 1970.

Harnack, Adolf von. *What is Christianity?* Reprint ed. New York: Harper & Row, 1957.

Harvey, Van A. "Meaning and Method . . . (Review)," *Religious Studies Review* 1, no. 1 (September 1975) : 13–19.

Hedenius, Ingemar. *Tro och ·etande.* Stockholm: Bonniers, 1949.

Kegley, Charles W., ed. *The Philosophy and Theology of Anders Nygren.* Carbondale, Ill.: Southern Illinois University Press, 1970.

Niebuhr, H. Richard. *The Meaning of Revelation.* New York: Macmillan, 1960.

Nygren, Anders. "Är evighetskategorien an religiös kategori?" *Kristendomen och vår tid* 17 (1922) : 220–41.

———. *Agape and Eros.* Philadelphia: Muhlenberg Press, 1953.

———. *Det bestående i kristendomen.* Religionsvetenskapliga skrifter, vol. 8. Stockholm: Sveriges kristliga studentrörelse, 1922.

———. *Christ and His Church.* Philadelphia: Westminster Press, 1956.

———. *The Church Controversy in Germany.* London: Student Christian Movement Press, 1934.

———. *Commentary on Romans.* Philadelphia: Muhlenberg Press, 1949.

———. "Corpus Christi." In *En bok om kyrkan.* Stockholm: Diakonistyrelsen, 1942.

———. "Corpus Christi." In *This is the Church.* Philadelphia: Muhlenberg Press, 1952.

———. *Dogmatikens vetenskapliga grundläggning.* Lund University årsskrift, New Series I, vol. 17, no. 8. Lund: Gleerup, 1922.

———. *Essence of Christianity.* London: Epworth Press, 1960.

———. *Etiska grundfrågor.* Stockholm. Sveriges kristliga studentrörelse, 1926.

———. *Filosofi och motivforskning.* Stockholm/Lund: Diakonistyrelsen, 1940.

———. *Filosofisk och kristen etik.* Lund University ärsskrift, New Series I, vol.18, no. 8. Lund: Gleerup, 1923.

———. *Försoningen, en gudsgärning.* Stockholm: Sveriges kristliga studentrörelse, 1932.

———. "From Atomism to Contexts of Meaning in Philosophy." In *Philosophical Essays Dedicated to Gunnar Aspelin.* Lund: Gleerup, 1963.

———. *The Gospel of God.* London: Student Christian Movement Press, 1951.

———. *Herdabrev till Lunds stift.* Stockholm: Diakonistyrelsen, 1949.

———. *Den kristna kärlekstanken genom tiderna.* 2 vols. Stockholm: Diakonistyrelsen, 1930–36.

———. *Kristus och hans kyrka.* Stockholm: Diakonistyrelsen, 1955.

———. *Luther's Doctrine of the Two Kingdoms.* Lausanne: WCC, 1948.

———. *Meaning and Method.* Philadelphia: Fortress Press, 1972.

———. "Den metafysiska filosofiens betydelse." *Bibelforskaren* 35 (1918) : 131–57.

———. *Pauli brev till Romarna.* Stockholm: Diakonistyrelsen, 1944.

———. *Det religionsfilosofiska grundproblemet.* Reprinted from *Bibelforskaren,* 1919–21. Lund: Gleerup, 1921.

———. *Religiöst apriori.* Lund: Gleerup, 1921.

———. *Religiösitet och kristendom.* Stockholm: Lindblad, 1926.

———. "The Religious Realm of Meaning." *The Christian Century* (July 16, 1958), pp. 823–26.

———. "The Role of the Self-Evident in History." *The Journal of Religion* 28, no. 4 (1948) : 235–41.

———. *The Significance of the Bible for the Church.* Philadelphia: Fortress Press, 1963.

———. "Till frågan om den transendentala metodens användbarhet inom religionsfilosofien." *Bibelforskaren* 40 (1923) : 273–93.

———. "Till frägan om teologiens objektivitet." In *Teologiska studier tillägnade Erik Stave, på 65-årsdagen.* Uppsala: Almqvist och Wiksell, 1922.

———. *Den tyska kyrkostriden.* Lund: Gleerup, 1934.

———. *Urkristendom och reformation.* Lund: Gleerup, 1932.

Runestam, Arvid. "Gudstro och självkännedom." In *Ordet och tron. Till Einar Billing på hans sextioårsdag.* Stockholm: Diakonistyrelsen, 1931.

Russell, Bertrand. *An Inquiry Into Meaning and Truth.* Atlantic Highlands, N.J.: Humanities, 1940.

Schleiermacher, Friedrich. *Die christliche Glaube.* 2 vols. Berlin: G. Reimer, 1821–22.

———. *The Christian Faith.* Edinburgh: T. & T. Clark, 1928.

Schweitzer, Albert. *The Quest of the Historical Jesus.* Reprint ed. New York: Macmillan, 1964.

Söderblom, Nathan. *Upperbarelsereligion.* Stockholm: Svenska Kyrkans Diakonistyrelses Bokförlag, 1930; also published as "Uppenbarelsereligionen," in *Skrifter i teologiska och kyrkliga ämnen tillägnade C. A. Toren.* Uppsala: Schultz, 1903.

Svenska män och kvinnor. Vol. 5. Stockholm: Bonniers, 1949.

Svensk teologisk kvartalskrift. Lund: Gleerup, 1925–.

Whitehouse, W. A. "Meaning and Method . . . (Review)." *Scottish Journal of Theology* 28 (1975): 576–77.

Wingren, Gustaf. *Theology in Conflict.* Philadelphia: Muhlenberg Press (1958).

———. "Was geschah eigentlich in Lund in den dreissiger Jahren?" *Theologische Literaturzeitung* 97, no. 12 (1972): 886–90.

Wittgenstein, Ludwig. *The Blue Book and Brown Books.* Oxford: Blackwell, 1958.

———. *Philosophical Investigations.* Oxford: Blackwell, 1958.

———. *Tractatus logico-philosophicus.* New York: Harcourt, Brace; London: Kegan Paul, 1922.